The Law of Whistleblowing

Transnational Crime

Volumes published in this Brill Research Perspective are listed at *brill.com/rptcs*

The Law of Whistleblowing

Cross-disciplinary, Contextual and Comparative Perspectives

Edited by

Valsamis Mitsilegas and Santiago Wortman Jofre

BRILL

LEIDEN | BOSTON

Library of Congress Control Number: 2021921324

Typeface for the Latin, Greek, and Cyrillic scripts: "Brill". See and download: brill.com/brill-typeface.

ISBN 978-90-04-45980-9 (paperback)
ISBN 978-90-04-45981-6 (e-book)

This book is printed on acid-free paper and produced in a sustainable manner.

Contents

Protecting Whistleblowers: The Challenges of Developing an Effective Legal Framework

Valsamis Mitsilegas and Santiago Wortman Jofre

Recent years have witnessed growing efforts at national and supranational level to develop legal frameworks to regulate whistleblowing. A number of new legislative instruments have been adopted to address specifically issues arising from whistleblowing, including the protection of whistleblowers – yet the legislative framework remains in flux, and the pace of change varies from state to state. Legislation addressing directly whistleblowing exists in tandem with measures addressing whistleblowing in a more indirect manner (including in the context of anti-corruption) or it gives way to efforts to address whistleblowing via existing legal and procedural avenues. Together with the question of how a specific legal framework on whistleblowing co-exists with existing general rules, comes the question of how whistleblower protection can be addressed effectively by different legal avenues and disciplines – from criminal to administrative to business to labour law. The present volume includes a wealth of contributions casting light on the evolving and multi-dimensional legal regime of whistleblower protection from a comparative perspective.

The opening chapter by Kafteranis is an in depth analysis of the new European Union framework on the protection of whistlebblowers. Kafteranis highlights the challenges faced by the EU in developing a comprehensive legal framework due to limits on EU powers and competence to legislate. He casts light on a number of challenges in the current law, including reaching a satisfactory and broad enough definition of whistleblowers and the limitations on reporting rules. Kafteranis points out the harmonising potential of EU law by stressing that the constitutionally mandated sectoral EU approach on whistleblowing may in effect become transversal in the implementation process. The aspect of implementation is also highlighted by Damaskou and Baltas in their contribution on the evolution of whistleblowing law in Greece. They highlight the transformative potential of the new EU legislation if it is implemented ambitiously in the domestic legal order. Their contributions maps the evolution of measures to protect whistleblowers from the stage before specific legislation to the adoption of a series of measures as part of the implementation of international (UN, Council of Europe, OECD) anti-corruption commitments by Greece. The authors appear to place faith in internationalisation and

 | DOI:10.1163/9789004459816_002

Europeanisation as a catalyst for domestic law reform, although they highlight persistent shortcomings on the ground.

The chapter by Yosef highlights the evolution of another domestic approach on whistleblowers' protection, this time in Israel. The contribution emphasises the benefits of a cross-disciplinary and cumulative approach, consisting of the application of multiple layers of legal protection – in criminal law, in labour law, and in administrative/civil service law. The potential and the limits of administrative redress mechanisms including via the intervention of the Ombudsman are highlighted. The author stresses the importance of an effective legal framework on internal reporting within organisations and the perspective of whislteblowers as victims of crime. The final chapter of this volume by Wortman Jofre and Rivero is a fascinating analysis of Argentina, whose legal system does not contain specific legislation on whistleblowers' protection. In the absence of such a specific framework, they make a powerful case for the extension of the rules on cooperating witnesses to protect whistleblowers. They highlight a number of key legal challenges underpinning effective protection of whistleblowers, including respecting fair trial and due process rights.

In their richness and complementarity, the chapters in this volume expertly focus on the key challenges in developing an effective regime on the protection of whistleblowers. They raise questions of which areas of law and legal disciplines (criminal law, labour law, administrative law among others) are best placed to provide effective protection, and whether a multi-level complementary approach is the best way forward. Each of the chapters brings into the fore the need to reach legal certainty on key aspects of whistleblower protection regimes – most notably, to adopt a reasonably broad definition of who is protected as a whistleblower, to provide meaningful protection of whistleblowers' fundamental rights, and to achieve effective internal reporting in organisations. From a comparative perspective, the contributions make us appreciate the context-specific evolution of whistleblowing law in different states and regions, and raises the question of the extent to which international and EU efforts can generate a meaningful global and regional level – playing field. An emphasis on monitoring, implementation and international dialogue will be key to achieve this goal.

From Obscurity to Limelight: Whistleblowers' Protection under EU Law

Dimitrios Kafteranis

The new Directive on the protection of whistleblowers responds to a continuing demand of the European Parliament for an EU legal framework on their protection. The Directive sets common minimum standards and brings a new era for the EU whistleblowers. Permanent issues such as the definition, the channels for disclosures and the protection are given an EU solution. Nonetheless, the Directive has certain points that need further analysis such as its legal basis and its relation to the criminal law. The present contribution aims to shed some light on these points that may be problematic in the near future.

1 Introduction: Blowing the Whistle at the Heart of the European Union

This essay will analyse in which way the issue of whistleblowing went from the obscurity to the limelight at the EU level. To this aim, the rocky path for adopting the Directive on the protection of whistleblowers will be explained together with particular remarks on this new EU legal framework. Special attention will be paid to the relationship between whistleblowing and criminal law.

Whistleblowing is not a new phenomenon for the European Union (EU).[1] From its very early years of the – then called – European Communities (EC) experienced cases of whistleblowing. Two cases will be analysed as an introduction to the theme of whistleblowing at the EU level: the first one is the case of Stanley Adams (1973) and the second one is the case of Paul van Buitenen. The interest for presenting the case of Stanley Adams lies on the fact that it is viewed as one of the first and most important case of whistleblowing at the EU level.[2] The second one, that of Paul van Buitenen, is a more recent case and its

1 Vincent Cador, La fonction publique européenne à l'épreuve du whistleblowing (2014) 1 R.A.E-L.A.E 119–120.

2 James Gobert and Maurice Punch, Whistleblowers, the public interest, and the Public Interest Disclosure Act 1998 (2000) 63 The Modern Law Review 25–54, 36.

 | DOI:10.1163/9789004459816_003

interest resides on the fact that, because of his whistleblowing, the members of the European Commission had to step down.[3]

Stanley Adams was an employee of the Swiss pharmaceutical company "Hoffmann La Roche". Adams, having a successful career in the company, obtained a senior position in the hierarchy of "Hoffmann La Roche". Being in this high-level position, he discovered that certain wrongdoings were happening. His company was engaged in anti-competitive practices such as the fixation of the price of certain vitamins.[4] Whilst being loyal to his company, he took the decision to blow the whistle and he addressed himself to the competition authorities of the EC.[5] In exchange of the information he provided for demonstrating the anti-competitive practices of his company, he demanded anonymity and protection.[6]

The competition authorities of the EC were ineffective, and Adam's name was revealed. EC officials have authorised "Hoffman La Roche" to photocopy the documents they have obtained from Adams. When the employees of "Hoffmann La Roche" were photocopying the documents, they found out that Adams was the employee who provided the documents to the EC competition authorities.[7] Once his name was revealed, negative consequences rather than protection started to occur for Adams. He was prosecuted by the Swiss prosecutorial authorities with the charge of revealing confidential information to foreigners and also experienced a personal tragedy as his wife committed suicide when she learnt her husband was arrested.[8] in addition to the criminal proceedings in Switzerland, Adams entered into a legal dispute with the EC competition authorities when he asked for damages compensation for revealing his name. The Adams case is a good example that highlights the inexistent protection of whistleblowers at the time, and the need for a legal framework in the EU.[9]

---

3 William Kingston, What can we do about the civil service? (2001) 90 Studies 320–330, 325.

4 Gerald Vinten, Whistleblowing: the UK experience – part 1 (2003) Management decision 41/9 935, 935.

5 Gerald Vinten, Whistleblowing: the UK experience – part 1 (2003) Management decision 41/9 935, 936.

6 Terry Morehead Dworkin, Whistleblowing, MNCs, and Peace (2002) 35 Vand. J. Transnat'l L. 457, 469.

7 Terry Morehead Dworkin, Whistleblowing, MNCs, and Peace (2002) 35 Vand. J. Transnat'l L. 457, 469.

8 Gerald Vinten, Whistleblowing: the UK experience – part 1 (2003) Management decision 41/9 935, 936.

9 Terry Morehead Dworkin, Whistleblowing, MNCs, and Peace (2002) 35 Vand. J. Transnat'l L. 457, 469.

The second case is sadly famous. Paul van Buitenen is the whistleblower whose disclosures led to the resignation of the Jacques Santer European Commission. Van Buitenen was an auditor working for the European Commission's Financial Control Directorate in Brussels. In 1998, he came across to documents showing serious financial wrongdoing, mismanagement and fraud within the European Commission.[10] As a first step, he made use of the internal EC reporting structures in order to inform his superiors about the aforementioned wrongdoings. Unfortunately, these measures proved to be ineffective. Given the failure of internal reporting mechanisms, he decided to write a letter to the (at the time) President of the Green Party, Magda Aelvoet. Due to his reporting, a Committee of Independent Experts was established in order to investigate these allegations. A very short deadline – two months – was given to the Commission to complete the inquiry. The Committee started to work on January 1999 and their report proved the allegations of fraud, mismanagement and the failure of the Commissioners to supervise their departments.[11] All these revelations from Van Buitenen led Jacques Santer and his Commissioners to resign in 1999.[12]

Van Buitenen wrote a book while he was suspended from his workplace about his process of blowing the whistle and the significance of reporting in order to discover wrongdoings affecting public administration.[13] He went through different difficult moments until, finally, blowing the whistle. He was threatened with losing his job (as he was suspended), his computer access was limited, and his phone was tapped.[14] He believed that:

> Whistleblowing is not a crime. It ought to be thought of as an important part of a modern and open administrative culture. Open and transparent

10 Terry Morehead Dworkin, Whistleblowing, MNCs, and Peace (2002) 35 Vand. J. Transnat'l L. 457, 470.

11 Committee of Independent Experts, First Report on Allegations regarding Fraud, Mismanagement and Nepotism in the European Commission (1999) para 9.4.25. Both this report and the Committee's second report are available on: <www.europarl.eu/experts/> accessed on 15 October 2019. The incoming Commission published a series of Codes of Conduct and consultation papers on the need to reform the accountability system. These efforts culminated to the White Paper on European Governance. See: European Commission, European Governance: A White Paper, COM(2001) 428. Also: Damian Chalmers, Gareth Davies and Giorgio Monti, *European Union Law* (CUP, 3rd ed. 2014) 381.

12 William Kingston, What can we do about the civil service? (2001) 90 Studies 320–330, 325.

13 Paul van Buitenen, Blowing the whistle (London Politicos 2000).

14 William Kingston, What can we do about the civil service? (2001) 90 Studies 320–330, 325.

> organisations have nothing to fear from a whistleblower. Whistleblowing is not a "necessary evil". It is a guarantee against the persistence of structurally endemic fraud and irregularities. It is an illusion to think that stricter regulations and a perfect audit policy can wipe out all major irregularities. In my own practice as assistant auditor in the Commission, but also before I worked in Brussels, I have observed on many occasions that major breakthroughs in ongoing investigations could only be achieved with the assistance of responsible whistleblowing.[15]

In recent years, the issue of whistleblowing became topical. Cases multiplied both at international and European level. Among the most famous, we all know Edward Snowden and his revelations about the massive surveillance activities of American citizens, foreign governments, and even ordinary foreign citizens.[16] That case changed forever the perception of State surveillance raising awareness on the risks of digital society. In parallel, several scandals denounced by whistleblowers revealed the harsh reality of a globalised finance. The "Luxleaks" scandal and its consequences on the tax policies at the EU level. In addition, the leaks of "Paradise Papers" and the "Panama Papers".[17] Other high-profile scandals related to corporate fraud such as Enron or Worldcom. These are examples of the modern preminent role of whistleblowing in our society and, consequently, at the EU.[18]

These cases have shown the urgency of a legislative intervention to offer a European coherent legislative framework to whistleblowing and its consequences in terms of protection. The European Union first introduced whistleblowing in some specific cases, mostly in the banking and financial sector, and only recently added another to the puzzle with the introduction of the Directive on the protection of persons reporting breaches of Union law.[19] The process is still ongoing and the puzzle is not yet completed, lacking more

15 Ibid., 249.

16 Paul Szoldra, 'This is Everything Edward Snowden Revealed in One Year of Unprecedented Top-secret Leaks' (2016) BUSINESS INSIDER, <http://www.businessinsider.com/snowden-leaks-timeline-2016-9> accessed on 4 October 2019.

17 Tony Porter and Karsten Ronit, 'Whistleblowing as a new regulatory instrument in global governance: the case of tax evasion' (2018) 31 Cambridge Review of International Affairs 6, 537.

18 Connor Berkebile, 'The Puzzle of Whisteblower Protection Legislation: Assembling the Piecemeal' (2018) 28 Ind Int'l & Comp L Rev 1, 2.

19 Directive (EU) 2019/1937 of the European Parliament and of the Council of 23 October 2019 on the protection of persons who report breaches of Union law (https://eur-lex.europa.eu/legal-content/en/TXT/?uri=CELEX%3A32019L1937).

details on certain elements of the Directive such as the meaning of worker under EU law or the unprecedented number of legal bases of the Directive (thirteen). In addition, the Directive has not considered financial rewards and it has not been detailed on the anonymity regime.

The aim of the following section is to present the path prior to adopting the Directive and to analyse some criminal law related aspects of it. In the first part, the role of the European Parliament will be presented alongside the European Commission's work on the protection of whistleblowers. In the second part, some of the criminal law aspects of the Directive will be discussed and, in the final part, concluding remarks will be given.

2 The Role of the European Parliament towards the Adoption of an EU Legal Framework on the Protection of Whistleblowers

The European Parliament may be characterised as a significant actor that has put forward and advanced the discussion, at the EU level, on the protection of whistleblowers.[20] It had voted several resolutions regarding the legal status of whistleblowers under EU law. Thanks to the extensive powers conferred by the Lisbon Treaty, the European Parliament started to demand an EU legal framework on the protection of reporting persons.[21] This demand is, normally, expressed by means of a resolution.[22] The resolution is not a legally binding document but is viewed as an invitation of the European Parliament to the European Commission to present legislation on a specific subject matter.[23] The resolution, voted by the European Parliament, has its legal basis on the article 225 of the Treaty on the Functioning of the European Union (TFEU) and on article 133 of the European Parliament's rules of procedure.[24]

---

20 Dimitrios Kafteranis, 'Protection of Whistleblowers in the European Union: The Promising Parliament Resolution and the Challenge for the European Commission' (2017) Oxford Business Law Blog (OBLB), available on: <https://www.law.ox.ac.uk/business-law-blog/blog/2017/12/protection-whistleblowers-european-union-promising-parliament> accessed on 14 February 2021.

21 Georgia Georgiadou, The European Commission's proposal for strengthening whistle-blower protection (2018) 3 EUCRIM, 166.

22 Damian Chalmers, Gareth Davies and Giorgio Monti, *European Union law* (OUP, 2010) 86. See: Resolution of 24 October 2017 on legitimate measures to protect whistle-blowers acting in the public interest when disclosing the confidential information of companies and public bodies.

23 Damian Chalmers, Gareth Davies and Giorgio Monti, *European Union law* (OUP, 2010) 86.

24 Consolidated version of the Treaty on the functioning of the European Union, art. 225 (2012) OJEU C 326. European Parliament, Rules of Procedure (2017) art. 133 available on:

First, the European Parliament was calling for whistleblower's protection within a specific sector. For instance, in the Resolution of 15 December 2011 related to the mid-term review of the European strategy 2007–2012 on health and safety at work, the European Parliament asked from the European Commission:

> (…) to propose a directive protecting individuals who legitimately warn of OHS unacknowledged risks, notably by notifying the appropriate labour inspectorate; these individuals should be protected in order to prevent any pressure being exerted on them (threats of dismissal, etc.); calls in this regard on the Commission to put an end to blacklisting of such workers by making sure that such a violation of a fundamental labour right is prevented by means of effective, proportionate and dissuasive sanctions.[25]

Here the European Parliament demanded the protection of reporting persons within health and safety at work.[26] This proposition may be characterised as a sectoral provision for it aims to protect specific persons: and, not a horizontal where the focus is on the protection of whistleblowers in different sectors of EU interest. These calls for protection of reporting persons continued throughout different Resolutions voted by the European Parliament.[27]

The different scandals at the EU level and the central role whistleblowers played in them, influenced the European Parliament's politics and changed

<http://www.europarl.europa.eu/sides/getDoc.do?pubRef=-//EP//NONSGML+RULES-EP+20170116+0+DOC+PDF+V0//EN&language=EN>.

25 European Parliament, Resolution of 15 December 2011 on the mid-term review of the European strategy 2007–2012 on health and safety at work (2011/2147(INI)), P7_TA(2011)0589, para. 54.

26 Tania Racho, La possibilité d'un encadrement juridique des lanceurs d'alerte par l'Union Européenne (2016) 10 Revue des Droits de l'Homme, 6.

27 European Parliament, Resolution of 23 October 2013 on organised crome, corruption, and money laundering (2013/2107(INI)), P7_TA(2013)0444 where it stated: "to submit, by the end of 2013, a legislative proposal establishing an effective and comprehensive European whistle-blower protection programme in the public and private sector to protect those who detect inefficient management and irregularities and report cases of national and cross-border corruption relating to EU financial interests and to protect witnesses, informers, and those who cooperate with the courts, and in particular witnesses testifying against mafia-type and other criminal organisations, with a view to resolving the difficult conditions under which they have to live (from risks of retaliation to the breakdown of family ties or from being uprooted from their home territory to social and professional exclusion); calls also on the Member States to put in place appropriate and effective protection for whistleblowers".

its stance about EU legislation on the protection of reporting persons.[28] Following these scandals, there was a pressing need for more transparency at the EU level which entailed the adoption of legislation on the protection of whistleblowers.[29] Thus the following resolutions mirrored the change of the European Parliament as they demanded a European legal framework on the protection of whistleblowers in every sector of EU interest. For instance, the Resolution of 25 November 2015 on tax rulings and other measures similar in nature or effect, proposed:

> (…) by June 2016, an EU legislative framework for the effective protection of whistleblowers and stressed that it is not acceptable that citizens and journalists can be subject to prosecution rather than legal protection when, acting in the public interest, they disclose information or report suspected misconduct, wrongdoing, fraud or illegal activity, in particular in cases of tax avoidance, tax evasion and money laundering, or any other conduct infringing the fundamental principles of the EU, such as the principle of sincere cooperation.[30]

The European Parliament started to leave behind the sectoral specific demands on the protection of whistleblowers and moved towards a pan sectoral protection covering different areas of interest and focusing only on the need to adopt a general legal framework on the protection of whistleblowers.[31] In this spirit, different resolutions were voted such as the Resolution of 16 December 2015 about transparency coordination and convergence to corporate tax policies or the Resolution of 6 July 2016 related to tax rulings and other measures similar in nature or effect.[32] Contrary to the demands of the European Parliament, the European Commission was not willing to propose any legislation on the

---

28 Georgia Georgiadou, The European Commission's proposal for strengtening whistleblower protection (2018) 3 EUCRIM, 166.

29 Simone White, A matter of life or death – whistleblowing legislation in the EU (2018) 3 EUCRIM, 171. See also: European Council, A new Strategic Agenda 2019–2024, available on: <https://www.consilium.europa.eu/media/39914/a-new-strategic-agenda-2019-2024.pdf> accessed on 30 October 2019 where transparency is identified as a key area of focus.

30 European Parliament, Resolution of 25 November 2015 on tax rulings and other measures similar in nature or effect (2015/2066(INI)), P8_TA(2015)0408, paras 144–145.

31 Simone White, A matter of life or death – whistleblowing legislation in the EU (2018) 3 EUCRIM, 171.

32 European Parliament, Resolution of 16 December 2015 on bringing transparency, coordination and convergence to corporate tax policies in the Union (2015/2010(INL)), P8_TA(2015)0457, recommendation A7. European Parliament, Resolution of 6 July 2016

protection of whistleblowers.[33] For instance, when the Resolution of 23 October 2013 was voted by the European Parliament in relation to organised crime and corruption, whistleblower's protection was included.

Despite the initiative of the European Parliament, the European Commission answered that it was not going to move forward the proposal. The European Commission attributed the weaknesses of whistleblowers' protection to a lack of implementation of existing international standards such the United Nations Convention against Corruption (UNCAC).[34] Despite the European's Commission stubborn refusal to answer to the resolutions, the European Parliament continued to demand EU legislation on the protection of whistleblowers.

The Resolution of 24 October 2017 on legitimate measures to protect whistleblowers acting in the public interest when disclosing the confidential information of companies and public bodies was the cornerstone towards the adoption of an EU Directive on the protection of whistleblowers.[35] This time the resolution only focused on the whistleblower and his or her protection. It stressed out the need for a specific EU legal framework that will protect

---

on tax rulings and other measures similar in nature of effect (2016/2038(INI)), P8_TA(2016)0310, paras 44–46.

33 Simone White, A matter of life or death – whistleblowing legislation in the EU (2018) 3 EUCRIM, 171–172. Some whistleblowing provisions were existent in the EU banking and financial legislation such as for market abuse, money laundering or trade secrets but they are not comprehensive and they are sector specific. European Union, Directive 2014/57 of 16 April 2014 on criminal sanctions for market abuse, OJ L 173, 179–189. European Union, Directive 2015/849 of 20 May 2015 on the prevention of the use of the financial system for the purposes of money laundering or terrorist financing, OJ L 141, 73–117. European Union, Directive 2016/943 of 8 June 2016 on the protection of undisclosed know-how and business information (trade secrets) against their unlawful acquisition, use and disclosure, OJ L 157, 1–18.

34 Alexandra Webster, 'Developments in Whistleblowing' (2015) 16 Business Law Journal 1, 72. United Nations Convention against Corruption (UNCAC), adopted on 31 October 2003, entered into force 14 December 2005, 186 signatories, available on: <https://www.unodc.org/unodc/en/corruption/uncac.html> accessed 30 August 2019.

35 European Parliament Resolution of 24 October 2017 on legitimate measures to protect whistle-blowers acting in the public interest when disclosing the confidential information of companies and public bodies (2016/2224(INI)) available on: <http://www.europarl.europa.eu/sides/getDoc.do?type=TA&language=EN&reference=P8-TA-2017-0402> accessed on 10 October 2019.

whistleblowing in every area of EU interest.[36] The Resolution emphasised the important role of whistleblowers in discovering illegalities and the way in which this will be beneficial for many sectors of EU interest.[37] The European Parliament invited the European Commission to present an horizontal EU legal framework on the protection of whistleblowers by the end of 2017. This time the European Commission accepted the invitation and presented the Proposal for a Directive on the protection of persons reporting breaches of Union law.[38]

3 From the Proposal to the Final Text of the Directive on the Protection of Persons Who Report Breaches of Union

On 23 April 2018, the European Commission presented its proposal for a Directive on the protection of persons reporting violations to the laws of the Union.[39] Answering the invitation of the European Parliament, the European Commission conducted a public consultation in order to listen to the different opinions and options before presenting its proposal.[40] The public consultation was completed by publishing an impact assessment on the protection of

36 European Parliament Resolution of 24 October 2017 on legitimate measures to protect whistle-blowers acting in the public interest when disclosing the confidential information of companies and public bodies (2016/2224(INI)), para 1, available on: <http://www.europarl.europa.eu/sides/getDoc.do?type=TA&language=EN&reference=P8-TA-2017-0402> accessed on 10 October 2019.

37 European Parliament Resolution of 24 October 2017 on legitimate measures to protect whistle-blowers acting in the public interest when disclosing the confidential information of companies and public bodies (2016/2224(INI)), point E, available on: <http://www.europarl.europa.eu/sides/getDoc.do?type=TA&language=EN&reference=P8-TA-2017-0402> accessed on 10 October 2019.

38 European Commission, Proposal for a directive of the European Parliament and of the Council on the protection of persons reporting breaches of Union law COM(2018) 218 final, available on: <https://ec.europa.eu/info/sites/info/files/placeholder_8.pdf> accessed on 10 May 2018.

39 European Commission, Proposal for a directive of the European Parliament and of the Council on the protection of persons reporting breaches of Union law COM(2018) 218 final, available on: <https://ec.europa.eu/info/sites/info/files/placeholder_8.pdf> accessed on 10 May 2018.

40 European Commission, Summary results of the public consultation on whistleblower protection, available on: <https://www.google.com/url?sa=t&rct=j&q=&esrc=s&source=web&cd=2&ved=2ahUKEwib44G-io7gAhUMU1AKHeSuBT8QFjABegQICRAC&url=http%3A%2F%2Fec.europa.eu%2Fnewsroom%2Fjust%2Fdocument.cfm%3Fdoc_id%3D47885&usg=AOvVaw2STppd4E-haqCot2HyNfuk> accessed on 25 October 2019.

whistleblowers prepared by the European Commission.[41] The proposal was an innovative and interesting text on the international standards of the protection of whistleblowers.[42]

Based on the proposal, negotiations followed between the European Parliament and the Council in order to find consensus on different issues such as the hierarchy of reporting channels.[43] In mid-March 2019, the Parliament and the Council reached an agreement about the Directive and it was published on the Official Journal of the EU on the 23 October 2019.[44] The adoption of the Directive is a significant step towards a better protection of whistleblowers at the EU level as well as a change of culture as the whistleblower starts to become an accepted figure. The final text of the Directive presents interesting points with the most important being the definition, the channels for disclosure, and the protection. In the following parts of this chapter, the purpose is to sketch out these points, emphasising the relation between criminal law and the whistleblower.

4 Remarks on the Directive and Its Special Relationship with Criminal Law

4.1 *The Quest for a Legal Basis*[45]

The Directive has several legal bases in an effort to encompass all the different EU areas of interest which are covered by it. The Treaty of Lisbon did not have a specific legal basis which could have allowed to regulate whistleblowing

41 European Commission, Commission Staff Working Document, Impact Assessment accompanying the document of the proposal for a Directive of the European Parliament and of the Council on the protection of persons reporting on breaches of Union law COM(2018) 218 final, available on: <https://eur-lex.europa.eu/legal-content/EN/TXT/PDF/?uri=CELEX:52018SC0116&from=EN> accessed on 26 October 2018.

42 Council of Europe, Recommendation CM/Rec(2014)7, Protection of whistle-blowers, adopted by the Committee of Ministers, 30 April 2014.

43 Council of the European Union, Proposal for a Directive of the European Parliament and of the Council on the protection of persons reporting breaches of Union law: progress report, February 2019, 4.

44 Directive (EU) 2019/1937 of the European Parliament and of the Council of 23 October 2019 on the protection of persons who report breaches of Union law, OJ L 395, 26.11.2019.

45 The present part of the Chapter focuses on the articles of the EU Treaties that were used in order to adopt the Directive on the protection of whistleblowers. When referring to "legal basis", it is meant a specific article that allows or not the adoption of an EU legal act. When using the "legal bases", it is understood the different articles used in order to adopt the EU legislative act.

at the EU level under this provision.[46] Consequently, and as it is established case-law, the European Commission made use of several legal bases which are indissociably linked without one being secondary and indirect in relation to the others, and only if they do not entail incompatible decision-making procedures.[47] Despite the use of several legal bases for the Directive, one of the main focuses is the protection of the internal market and the protection of the financial interests of the EU.[48] The choice of using several legal bases was criticized by a minority of Member States but they were unsuccessful in amending that.[49]

Turning to the criminal law basis, the Directive proposal does not contain any such legal basis. The European Commission has decided not to make use of the Treaties' articles that are related to criminal law. Although in its impact assessment, the European Commission referred to the need to combat criminal law related offences such as corruption and fraud, it decided that there was no self-standing basis in the Treaties and, indirectly, did not mention anything about using them in the several legal bases used.[50] The issue of using the criminal law articles as legal bases for the Directive was suggested by the European Parliament when presenting its comments on the Directive proposal. The opinion of the Committee on Legal Affairs of the European Parliament and the

---

46 European Commission, Commission Staff Working Document, Impact Assessment accompanying the document of the proposal for a Directive of the European Parliament and of the Council on the protection of persons reporting on breaches of Union law COM(2018) 218 final, 30–31, available on: <https://eur-lex.europa.eu/legal-content/EN/TXT/PDF/?uri=CELEX:52018SC0116&from=EN> accessed on 30 October 2019.

47 Judgments of 6 November 2008 in *Parliament* v *Council*, C-155/07, EU:C:2008:605, paragraph 37; and of 3 September 2009 in *Parliament* v *Council*, C-166/07, EU:C:2009:499, paragraphs 68 and 69.

48 European Commission, Commission Staff Working Document, Impact Assessment accompanying the document of the proposal for a Directive of the European Parliament and of the Council on the protection of persons reporting on breaches of Union law COM(2018) 218 final, 30–31, available on: <https://eur-lex.europa.eu/legal-content/EN/TXT/PDF/?uri=CELEX:52018SC0116&from=EN> accessed on 30 October 2019.

49 Parliament of the United Kingdom, European Scrutiny Committee, Whistleblowing and breaches of EU law (2019), available on: <https://publications.parliament.uk/pa/cm201719/cmselect/cmeuleg/301-lxx/30104.htm> accessed on 13 October 2019, point 1.9.

50 European Commission, Commission Staff Working Document, Impact Assessment accompanying the document of the proposal for a Directive of the European Parliament and of the Council on the protection of persons reporting on breaches of Union law COM(2018) 218 final, 30–31, available on: <https://eur-lex.europa.eu/legal-content/EN/TXT/PDF/?uri=CELEX:52018SC0116&from=EN> accessed on 30 October 2019.

opinion of the Legal Service of the Council of the European Union shed light on the issue of criminal law basis of the Directive.[51]

Following the adoption of the Lisbon Treaty, the Union's criminal law competence was expanded.[52] Under the new powers, Article 83 TFEU becomes the legal basis for the approximation of substantive criminal law. Despite these new provisions, the debate is ongoing about the exact limits of the Union's competence.[53] Regarding the adoption of the Directive on the protection of whistleblowers, the European Union preferred not to make use of Article 83 TFEU. This refusal to use Article 83 deserves to be commented as it may be an issue in relation to the right choice of a legal basis if a case challenging the legal basis of the Directive will appear in front of the Court of Justice of the European Union.

Article 83(1) TFEU has specific areas where the competence is given in order to

> (…) establish minimum rules concerning the definition of criminal offences and sanctions in the areas of particularly serious crime with a cross-border dimension resulting from the nature or impact of such offences or from a special need to combat them on a common basis.[54]

It is certain that the Directive could not have used Article 83(1) TFEU as it does not establish minimum rules concerning a criminal offence as explained above. Article 83(2) TFEU is more interesting to that extent. Article 83(2) TFEU has as its purpose is to approximate criminal law when it "(…) *proves essential to ensure the effective implementation of a Union policy in an area which has been subject to harmonisation measures*".[55]

---

51 European Parliament, Committee on Legal Affairs, Opinion on the legal basis for the proposal for a directive of the European Parliament and the Council on the protection of persons reporting on breaches of Union law (2018), available on: <http://www.europarl.europa.eu/doceo/document/JURI-AL-629554_EN.pdf> accessed on 14 October 2019. Council of the European Union, Opinion of the legal service on the legal basis for the proposal for a directive on the protection of persons reporting on breaches of Union law (2018) JUR_14620/18.

52 Treaty on the Functioning of the European Union. OJ C 326.

53 Valsamis Mitsilegas, *EU Criminal Law After Lisbon. Rights, Trust and the Transformation of Justice in Europe* (Oxford and Portland, Oregon: Hart Publishing, 2016) 4–5, 19–21, 53–68.

54 These offences are listed as such: terrorism, trafficking in human beings and sexual exploitation of women and children, illicit drug trafficking, illicit arms trafficking, money laundering, corruption, counterfeiting of means of payment, computer crime and organised crime. There is the possibility to add others in the list by unanimous decision of the Council and the consent of the European Parliament.

55 Consolidated version of the Treaty on the functioning of the European Union, art. 83(2) (2012) OJEU C 326.

In the case of the Directive, harmonisation measures are adopted towards the legal protection of whistleblowers at the EU level. The whistleblower is an enforcement tool who has to report wrongdoings of criminal nature (apart from civil or administrative or any other type). In fact, the whistleblower has to report criminal offences such as money laundering. The whistleblower is a crime-fighting measure and it would be desirable to have Article 83(2) TFEU as a legal basis. At first sight, it is not possible to use Article 83(2) TFEU as a legal basis for the adoption of the Directive. However, the fact that the Directive harmonises whistleblower protection and demands the creation of a criminal immunity seems to harmonise criminal laws in order to effectively implement the protection of the whistleblower as a Union's policy.

The aforementioned concept of a crime-fighting measure has already been put in front of the Luxembourg Court where the Court gives priority to the protection of internal market or other policies rather than the criminal law.[56] The Court demonstrates, often, its strong preference for Union friendly legal basis rather than the criminal law basis which are more national friendly.[57] The Court prefers, by applying its "main aim" doctrine, that if the predominant component of a measure favours a non-AFJS (Area of Freedom, Security and Justice) legal basis, this basis must be given priority over an AFJS legal basis.[58] For the Directive on the protection of whistleblowers, the central legal basis is Article 114 TFEU and the other legal bases are complementary to it.[59] The need to protect the internal market is one of the reasons to adopt this Directive and Article 114 TFEU, as a legal basis, has a more fertile ground because of its wide acceptance as a proper legal basis and for its ordinary legislative procedure.[60] The procedural obstacles of Article 83 TFEU led to its refusal as a legal basis.

The Committee of the Parliament stated that while in Article 83(1) and 83(2) TFEU the ordinary legislative procedure is applied, its paragraph three (3) contains an "emergency brake" provision where Member States can refer a file to

---

56 *Ireland v Parliament and Council* (C-301/06) EU:C: 2009:68.
Commission v Council (environmental sanctions) (C-176/03) EU:C: 2005:542, paras 38–53.
Commission v Council (ship-source pollution) (C-440/05) EU:C: 2007:625, paras 52–74.
Commission v Council (C-137/12) EU:C: 2013:675, paras 70–72.

57 E. Herlin-Karnell, 'Annotation, Case Comment Case C-301/06, Ireland v. Parliament and Council' (2009) 46 C.M.L. Rev. 1667.

58 Jacob Oberg, 'The Legal Basis for EU Criminal Law Harmonisation: A Question of Federalism?' (2018) 43(3) European Law Review 366, 375.

59 Vigjilenca Abazi, 'The European Union Whistleblower Directive: A Game Changer for Whistleblowing Protection?' (2020) Industrial Law Journal 1, 7.

60 *Commission v Council (Titanium Dioxide)* (C-300/89) EU:C: 1991:244, paras 22–25.
Commission v Council (C-338/01) EU:C: 2004:25.
Commission v Council (C-155/91) EU:C: 1993:98, paras 19–21.

the European Council.[61] Therefore, Article 83 cannot be combined with other legal bases as they will entail incompatible decision making mechanisms.[62] In addition, measures adopted under Article 83 TFEU will only apply to Ireland if it opts in (Protocol No 21) and they will not apply to Denmark (Protocol No 22). Although this event will not be an obstacle in relation to the legislative procedure, it will create a possible split in the Council. Different Member States will participate to different parts of the Directive and this would be problematic for the discussions and negotiations.[63] The Legal Service of the Council of the European Union followed the reasoning of the Committee of the Parliament in relation to the criminal law legal basis.[64]

The whistleblower is an enforcement tool created to enforce EU law and this enforcement tool is beneficial also to the enforcement of EU legislation aiming to detect criminal offences.[65] The need for an enforcement tool within the Directive, could have inspired the use of Article 83 TFEU or the adoption of another EU legal instrument on the criminal law aspects. The choice of not using Article 83 TFEU because of the procedural obstacles it would create is, although, a reasonable decision.[66]

4.2 *The Material Scope of the Directive*

The choice of the legal bases is related to the scope of the Directive and which are the areas of EU interest. The Directive provides for protection only when

61 European Parliament, Committee on Legal Affairs, Opinion on the legal basis for the proposal for a directive of the European Parliament and the Council on the protection of persons reporting on breaches of Union law (2018), 10, available on: <http://www.europarl.europa.eu/doceo/document/JURI-AL-629554_EN.pdf> accessed on 14 October 2019. Council of the European Union, Opinion of the legal service on the legal basis for the proposal for a directive on the protection of persons reporting on breaches of Union law (2018) JUR_14620/18.

62 European Parliament, Committee on Legal Affairs, Opinion on the legal basis for the proposal for a directive of the European Parliament and the Council on the protection of persons reporting on breaches of Union law (2018), 10, available on: <http://www.europarl.europa.eu/doceo/document/JURI-AL-629554_EN.pdf> accessed on 14 October 2019.

63 European Parliament, Committee on Legal Affairs, Opinion on the legal basis for the proposal for a directive of the European Parliament and the Council on the protection of persons reporting on breaches of Union law (2018), 10, available on: <http://www.europarl.europa.eu/doceo/document/JURI-AL-629554_EN.pdf> accessed on 14 October 2019.

64 Council of the European Union, Opinion of the legal service on the legal basis for the proposal for a directive on the protection of persons reporting on breaches of Union law (2018) JUR_14620/18, 21.

65 Dimitrios Kafteranis, 'A new enforcement tool: a Directive to protect whistle-blowers' (2020) 41 Business Law Review 50.

66 Samuli Miettinen, 'Criminal competence and the choice of legal basis: space in the margins?' (2015) 5 European Criminal Law Review 2, 225–226 discussing the procedural obstacles that Article 83 creates.

one of the chosen areas of EU interest are at stake. The reported breach should be relevant to these areas as given in Article 2 of the Directive in order to receive the full protection of the EU.[67] These areas are: public procurement, financial services, product and transport safety, protection of the environment, nuclear safety, food and feed safety, animal welfare, public health, consumer protection, protection of privacy and personal data, protection of the internal market including the competition and State aid rules, and corporate tax regimes which may defeat the purpose of the applicable corporate tax law.

The Directive leaves the possibility to the Member States to extend the protection under national law to the areas not covered by the EU legislation.[68] Despite the broad areas of EU interest for which a report can be made, the Directive was characterised as providing sectoral protection.[69] It was also criticised because it may create two different national legislations: one transposing the Directive and one related to what falls outside the material scope of the Directive, thus issues related to national law.[70]

First, the Directive is characterised as an EU sectoral approach and not as a horizontal legal framework.[71] Literature shows different opinions of this EU approach to whistleblowing.[72] From a first perspective, this choice is understandable in the light of the missing legal basis under the Treaties. The European Union did not have a legal basis that could cover whistleblowers' protection in every sector of interest. For this reason, it opted for a sector specific approach where it covers areas of EU interest. From a different angle, one might observe that this approach fits the limited competences of the EU. It did not have the choice to expand the Directive as these sectors represent its

67 Directive, art. 2(1).

68 Directive, art. 2(2).

69 Simone White, A matter of life or death – whistleblowing legislation in the EU (2018) 3 EUCRIM, 171–172. Veronika Nad and Naomi Colvin, Whistleblowing in the European Union: a new Directive to protect citizens, democracy and rule of law, blueprint for free speech, 2019, p. 2.

70 Dimitrios Kafteranis and Robert Brockhaus, 'No more Piecemeal Tactics – call for a comprehensive implementation of EU's Whistleblowing Directive' (2020) Verfassungsblog on matters constitutional, available on: <https://verfassungsblog.de/no-more-piecemeal-tactics/> accessed on 14 February 2021.

71 Simone White, A matter of life or death – whistleblowing legislation in the EU (2018) 3 EUCRIM, 171–172.

72 Emanuela Andreis, 'Towards common minimum standards for whistleblower protection across the EU' (2019) 4(2) European Papers 575, 577–578 available on: <http://www.europeanpapers.eu/en/europeanforum/towards-common-minimum-standards-for-whistleblower-protection-across-eu> accessed on 15 November 2019.

competences. As the Legal Service of the Council characterised it, it is a cumulative sectoral or "omnibus" approach.[73]

The European Union adopted an horizontal legal framework considering its limited competences.[74] There is no point arguing that the EU legal framework is sectoral as the EU could not cover areas where it has no competence.[75] As a result, the Directive is an horizontal legal act on the protection of whistleblowers limited under the competences of the European Union. It is the duty of the Member States to examine if they should extend the scope of the Directive on issues covered only by national law.[76]

It is interesting to provide some more analysis on the concept of a sectoral approach legislation towards the protection of whistleblowers. A sectoral approach means that different whistleblower's protection provisions

---

73 Council of the European Union, Opinion of the legal service on the legal basis for the proposal for a directive on the protection of persons reporting on breaches of Union law (2018) JUR_14620/18, 3.

74 The impact assessment of the European Commission had found that the EU Treaties cannot provide for a specific legal basis to regulate the legal position of whistleblowers, at the EU level, in general. The right to freedom of expression, as enshrined in the Charter of Fundamental Rights of the EU, would have been a legal basis for a horizontal approach but it cannot serve as standalone legal basis. European Commission, Commission Staff Working Document, Impact Assessment accompanying the document of the proposal for a Directive of the European Parliament and of the Council on the protection of persons reporting on breaches of Union law COM(2018) 218 final, 30–31, available on: <https://eur-lex.europa.eu/legal-content/EN/TXT/PDF/?uri=CELEX:52018SC0116&from=EN> accessed on 26 October 2018.

75 The EU is bound to the principal of conferral. In addition, reportable wrongdoing can only apply in areas where Member States have previously agreed on sharing competences. Paul Craig and Grainne de Burca, EU law – text, cases and materials – (OUP, 6th ed., 2015) 75. Veronika Nad and Naomi Colvin, Whistleblowing in the European Union: a new Directive to protect citizens, democracy and rule of law, blueprint fro free speech, 2019, p. 2.

76 The French Senate has issued its concerns on this issue it gave its opinion on the Proposal for a Directive protecting persons reporting breaches of Union law. The French Senate stated that even though the Directive has a limited scope of application (only to wrongdoings related to EU law), its transposition will result in a problem of harmonisation as France will be "obliged" to amend its existing legislation in order to avoid the co-existence of two different legal frameworks for the protection of whistleblowers. Sénat, Rapport fait sur la proposition de directive sur la protection des personnes dénoncent les infractions au droit de l'Union (2018) N° 638, 8. Dimitrios Kafteranis and Robert Brockhaus, 'No more Piecemeal Tactics – call for a comprehensive implementation of EU's Whistleblowing Directive' (2020) Verfassungsblog on matters constitutional, available on: <https://verfassungsblog.de/no-more-piecemeal-tactics/> accessed on 15 February 2021.

are spread across a number of different legal acts.[77] This means that whistleblowers are protected when they report something specific. For instance, there is a specific provision under the EU Regulation on Market Abuse which allows people to report to the competent authorities in relation to insider dealing and market manipulation.[78] Other sectoral provisions relate to the banking supervision or money laundering legislation.[79] On the contrary, an horizontal legislation has as a core element the protection of whistleblowers in every possible area of interest, which may be also called as a pan sectoral legislation.[80] The purpose of the horizontal legislation is to provide the legal framework of the protection of whistleblowers in every field of interest. This is what the EU did, although limited to its areas of interest. For the EU to limit the whistleblower's protection to EU areas of interest is a question of competence, not choice.

4.3 *The Definition of Whistleblowers under the EU Directive*

The definition of the whistleblower is widely debated in the legal literature.[81] The legislative answers diverge, and a common uniform definition does not exist. Clearly, it is important to be able to describe and recognise a whistleblower in order to be able to offer them appropriate protection. The EU Directive provides a common definition among Member States for a person who reports breaches of Union law, thus enabling protection under the Directive. The

77 Goverment Reform Unit, Department of Public Expenditure and Reform, Protected Disclosures Bill 2013 – regulatory impact analysis, July 2013, 10.

78 Regulation (EU) N° 596/2014 of the European Parliament and of the Council of 16 April 2014 on market abuse (market abuse regulation), O.J.E.U. L 173/1.

79 European Union, Directive 2015/849 of 20 May 2015 on the prevention of the use of the financial system for the purposes of money laundering or terrorist financing, OJ L 141, 73–117. European Union. Regulation No 468/2014 of the European Central Bank establishing the framework for cooperation within the Single Supervisory Mechanism between the European Central Bank and national competent authorities and with national designated authorities (SSM Framework Regulation), 16 April 2014.

80 The Final Report of the Tribunal of Inquiry into Certain Planning Matters and Payments (2012) 2644 available on: <http://www.planningtribunal.ie/images/finalReport.pdf> accessed on 23 October 2019.

81 Richard Haigh & Peter Bowal 'Whistleblowing and Freedom of Conscience: Towards a New Legal Analysis' (2012) Comparative Research in Law & Political Economy, Research Paper No. 1974982, 6–12. Janet P Miceli & Marcia P Near, "Organizational Dissidence: The Case of Whistle-Blowing" (1985) 4 J Bus Ethics 1, 4. Gerry Ferguson, Global Corruption – law, theory and practice (UVIC press, 3rd ed., vol. 1) 1009.s. David Banisar, "Whistleblowing: International Standards and Developments" in Irma E Sandoval, ed, Contemporary Debates on Corruption and Transparency: Rethinking State, Market, and Society (Washington, DC: World Bank, Institute for Social Research, UNAM, 2011) at 4, online: <http://ssrn.com/abstract_id=1753180>.

definition of whistleblowers broadly defines them as "workers" in the widest sense of the word.[82] The whistleblower may be an employee, either in the public or private sector, a trainee, a volunteer, a person in the hiring process; someone who no longer works in the identified place; a contractor; a subcontractor; or, a shareholder.[83] If the person fulfils this first requirement, then he or she has to reasonably believe that the fact he or she is reporting is true at the time the report is being made, and he or she has to respect the designated channels for disclosure.[84]

The Directive sets a low threshold of requirements in order to be able to label someone as a whistleblower. The Directive leaves aside requirements such as good faith or reporting in the public interest as it is for instance the case in the Irish legislation.[85] Nonetheless, this approach contradicts the French approach and the case law of the Strasbourg Court which the aforementioned requirements are necessary and relevant for protection.[86] The minimum requirements for protection imply that bad faith whistleblowers may be protected to the same extent as whistleblowers who reported wrong facts without being conscious of their mistake. The pressure from outside and inside the EU, mostly from the European Parliament, led to this "innovative" definition which, *prima facie*, seems to facilitate the protection of whistleblower and consequently the whole process of reporting.[87]

4.3.1 The Concept of the Self-Standing Criminal Offence

An additional requirement that the whistleblower has to respect in order to be labelled as such, is the non-existence of a self-standing criminal offence at the time of acquiring the relevant information.[88] In essence, the whistleblower should not commit a criminal offence such as the theft or trespassing when he or she gets the necessary information in order to blow the whistle. This point may be problematic as the whistleblower, by taking into account recent examples in Europe,[89] is often criminally charged either for theft or for

82 Directive (n.19) art. 4.

83 Ibid.

84 Directive (n.19) art. 6(1).

85 Protected Disclosures Act 2014, number 14 of 2014, ss. 1–3.

86 Law n° 2016–1691 of 6 December 2016 related to transparency, the fight against corruption and the modernization of economic life, JORF n°0287, art. 6. *Guja v. Moldova* App no 14277/04 (ECtHR 12 February 2008).

87 European Parliament Resolution (n 15) para 14.

88 Directive art. 21(3).

89 See to that end the Luxleaks case where the two whistleblowers were accused of theft and breach of professional secrecy.

breach of professional secrecy, *inter alia*. This requirement will be the Sword of Damocles hanging over the head of the whistleblower as on the one side, it is necessary to provide evidence which may be legally translated into theft or breach of secrecy duties. On the other hand, whistleblowers will not know if they can, finally, be protected under the Directive due to the ambiguity of the concept of the self-standing criminal offence and of the criminal immunity.[90]

The Directive provides some clarifications as to how the concept of a self-standing criminal offence should be understood. These clarifications are in the recitals of the Directive and not in the main text.[91] Recital 92 sheds some light to the concept of the self-standing criminal offence.[92] According to the Directive, whistleblowers have the possibility to make copies or remove documents from the premises of the organisation. The Directive refers to two types of criminal offences: physical trespassing and hacking. While it grants civil, administrative and labour-related immunity, it does not grant criminal immunity when the reporting persons acquires the information in an indirect way. This indirect way can be by accessing the e-mails of a co-worker or files which they normally do not use in the purpose of their work, by taking pictures of the premises or by entering to locations where normally they do not have the right to enter. By not granting criminal immunity, the criterion of the self-standing criminal offence will be fulfilled as the whistleblower will be criminally accused the time he or she acquires the information needed in order to report. Even if whistleblowers will not be held liable in terms of civil, administrative or labour law, they can be held criminally liable, thus creating an important gap regarding their protection.

In addition, with the advent of digitalisation, the working place has changed and the information is not mostly on paper form but in a digital one.[93] Consequently, the whistleblower may easily be criminally charged for accessing

---

TA Lux, 29 Juin 2016, n° 1981/2016.
CA Luxembourg, 15 Mars 2017, n° 117/17 X.
CSJ, cass., 11 Janvier 2018, n° 3911.
CSJ, cass., 11 Janvier 2018, n° 3912.

90 Veronika Nad and Naomi Colvin, Whistleblowing in the European Union: a new Directive to protect citizens, democracy and rule of law, blueprint for free speech, 2019, p. 4.

91 Directive, recitals 91 and 92.

92 Directive, recital 92.

93 Rachelle Bosua, Simon Milton, Suelette Dreyfus and Reeva Lederman, 'Going public: Researching external whistleblowing in a new media age' in A.J. Brown, David Lewis, Richard Moberly & Wim Vandekerckhove (eds), International research handbook on whistleblowing (Routledge 2014) 250.

digital information without permission.[94] This should be clarified and criminalisation should be limited to computer hacking when it is perpetrated for personal gain. If limited to computer hacking where necessary details will be given on this specific offence by the Directive, the whistleblower will feel certain about the risks related to taking the necessary information. More attention should be given to the concepts of acts or omissions that are unrelated or unnecessary to the specific reporting.[95]

It can be argued that the Directive desires to create a proportional safe net where the whistleblower should only access and report what is necessary. If there is a proportionality reason behind the concept of self-standing criminal offence, this should be made apparent. The proportional safe net is related to the idea that the whistleblower should provide only what it is necessary and no other information that is not connected to the reported breach. If this is the case, it should be made clearer by the Directive and the national legislations, transposing the Directive, that there is a proportionality check behind. The current wording creates confusion and uncertainty which may discourage a future whistleblower to report and may have legal ramifications. Finally, the Directive and the national implementing legislations should clarify if the whistleblower can be protected when he or she discloses the information whilst the prior act of acquiring or accessing the information is not protected. From the wording of the Directive, such a situation is possible as the concept of the self-standing criminal offence is related to the acquisition of the information and is distinct from the disclosure of the information. As a result, it may be the situation where the whistleblower would be criminally charged for the way he or she accessed the information but protected for his or her reporting. It is certain that this situation is not ideal and not reassuring for the whistleblower.

4.4 *Channels for Disclosure*

Turning to the channels for disclosures, the Directive presents a variation of the "three-tier" model for disclosure as adopted, for example, by the Irish and French legislation.[96] The tiered model proves for a hierarchy of reporting mechanisms from internal to external. The tendency at the European level is

---

94 Sylvain Waserman, 'Improving the protection of whistleblowers all over Europe' (2019) Council of Europe, Committee on Legal Affairs and Human Rights, 15.

95 Sylvain Waserman, 'Improving the protection of whistleblowers all over Europe' (2019) Council of Europe, Committee on Legal Affairs and Human Rights, 15.

96 Protected Disclosures Act 2014, number 14 of 2014, Ireland (the Irish legislation incentivises internal reporting). See also Robert G. Vaughn, The successes and failures of whistleblower laws (EE Publishing, 2012) 324–332.

to require internal whistleblowing first, and if not possible, whistleblowing to competent authorities. If reporting to the competent authorities is not a viable choice, then the employee can disclose the information directly to the public, meaning media, internet platforms or journals.[97]

The Directive adopts a similar model, although not identical. The same channels for disclosure exist but not the same strict hierarchical separation as to which channel the whistleblower should choose first. He or she can report either internally or directly to the authorities without the obligation to report internally first.[98] Reporting to the authorities can be the first option and he or she will have the same protection as if reporting internally. This point was debated during the negotiations between the European Parliament and the Council having this lenient approach towards reporting internally or externally, as final outcome.[99] Public disclosure remains the last solution for the whistleblower when the other two channels are not effective or responsive.[100] Public disclosure is a choice, but the protection is awarded only if strict conditions are met. However, there are two exceptions that allow the whistleblower to disclose the information directly to the public. One is the case of an imminent danger or irreversible damage if the disclosure does not happen immediately.[101] Regretfully, the Directive does not give any examples or definition of what may constitute an imminent danger or irreversible damage. This transforms the option of the public disclosure into an insecure and difficult choice for the whistleblower. The second is when the whistleblower considers that reporting to the competent authorities would be futile given the particular circumstances of the case.[102] These choices, if not correctly chosen, may lead to criminal or civil charges for him or such as the breach of his or her secrecy or confidentiality obligations.[103]

97 European Commission Proposal (n 16) and Recommendation CM/Rec(2014)7, Protection of whistle-blowers, adopted by the Committee of Ministers of the Council of Europe, 30 April 2014.

98 Directive (n.19) art. 6(1)(b).

99 See more on the following link: <https://www.whistleblowersblog.org/2019/03/articles/eu-whistleblowers/provisional-eu-law-to-protect-whistleblowers/> accessed on 30 July 2019.

100 Directive (n.19) art. 15.

101 Directive, art. 15(1)(b)(i).

102 Directive (n.19) art. 15(1)(b)(ii).

103 Dimitrios Kafteranis, 'Reporting to the Boss or the Authorities: the ongoing dilemma of the whistle-blower' (2018) Cambridge Law Review, pp. 17–20.

4.5 *Protection*

4.5.1 Labour Law Related Protection

The Directive offers important protective measures and advantages to the whistleblower. Firstly, and in order to be able to be granted protection under the Directive, the whistleblower has to respect the procedural path (as described above), he or she should have had a reasonable belief that the information reported was true at the time when reported and he or she did not commit a self-standing criminal offence.[104] If these conditions are met, then the whistleblower can enjoy protection under the Directive. As any piece of legislation on whistleblowing, protection from retaliation is the core point. The Directive invites Member States to take all the necessary measures in order to protect the whistleblower from any type of retaliation either direct or indirect.[105] To that end, the Directive provides a long, but not exhaustive, list of possible forms of retaliation.[106] In addition, the Directive calls on Member States to ensure that whistleblowers have access to different measures of support such as access to independent advice or legal aid in criminal proceedings.[107] The form of these measures is left to the discretion of the Member States.[108]

4.5.2 Criminal Immunity

The Directive aims at making the status of the whistleblower a waiver for any kind of liability.[109] It seeks to provide immunity if the person fulfils the criteria to be labelled as whistleblower. The Directive hands some details in the recitals 91 and 92 in relation to the concept of the criminal immunity, as it was the case for the concept of the self-standing criminal offence, and not in the main text. In an effort to ensure an enhanced protection for the whistleblower, the recitals provide some examples where criminal liability should be waived. First, the legal or contractual duties of individuals such as the duty of loyalty or confidentiality or any non-disclosure agreement, they should not be able to deny protection or to penalise the whistleblower *for having done so where providing the information falling within the scope of such clauses and agreements is necessary for revealing a breach.*[110] Apart from breaching the loyalty duties, the

104 Directive (n.19) art. 6(1)(a).
105 Directive (n.19) art. 19.
106 Ibid.
107 Directive (n.19) art. 20.
108 Veronika Nad and Naomi Colvin, Whistleblowing in the European Union: a new Directive to protect citizens, democracy and rule of law, blueprint for free speech, 2019, p. 3.
109 Directive (n.19) art. 21(2).
110 Directive, recital 91.

whistleblower should also have reasonable grounds to believe that reporting was necessary to reveal a breach under the scope of the Directive.[111]

The whistleblower should provide information only if he or she has "*reasonable grounds to believe that its reporting or disclosure was necessary*" for revealing a breach related to the Directive.[112] Any superfluous information reported by the whistleblower "*without having such reasonable grounds*", will dismiss any protection offered under the Directive.[113] Firstly, the whistleblower should have reasonable grounds to believe that the reported thing relates to a breach. It seems delicate to provide a definition of the concept of reasonable grounds as it may be either the fact that a normal citizen would have thought that there is a breach or a professional in the same position may have though the same.[114] Apart from the need to find the definition of "reasonable grounds", whistleblowers have to think if the reported behaviour fits under the reasonable grounds test and is an actual breach. If so, whistleblowers should be careful to select and give only the necessary information.

Furthermore, and apart from respecting the correct amount of information to be reported, whistleblowers have to pay attention to the way of acquiring the information.[115] Recital 92 provides certain cases where the way of acquiring the information is lawful. The most important is that whistleblowers have to have lawful access to the information. Thus, he or she can choose if it is necessary to copy or remove the information from the premises of the organisation. However, if the reporting person commits a criminal offence such as physical trespassing or hacking, he or she will be criminally liable under the relevant national laws. It is remarkable that there is a waiver of civil, administrative and labour liability if the reporting person accessed the e-mails of a co-worker or used files which normally do not fall under his or her work but he or she can be criminally liable.[116] This second requirement for the waiver of the criminal liability is synonym with the concept of the self-standing criminal offence.[117] If the whistleblower acquires unlawfully the information needed, it is for the national courts to decide upon his or her criminal liability.

---

111 Directive, recital 91.

112 Directive, recital 91.

113 Directive, recital 91.

114 Tom Devine who is a leading expert in whistleblowing research suggests that the reasonable belief should be analysed in light of what a person with equivalent knowledge, training and experience would agree. He demands that this definition should be transposed in all national laws. See: <https://www.whistleblower.org/blog/assessment-of-european-union-whistleblower-directive/> accessed on 12 October 2019.

115 Directive, recital 92.

116 Directive, recital 92.

117 Directive, article 21(3).

4.5.3 Relationship between the Concept of the Self-Standing Criminal Offence and Criminal Immunity under the Directive

The concept of criminal immunity presents an interesting relationship with the concept of the self-standing criminal offence. The whistleblower usually acquires the necessary information by breaching a rule, either of civil or of criminal nature. Consequently, depending on the national legal system, this breach may constitute a criminal offence for which the status of whistleblower under the Directive will not be able to act as a defence. As a result, the whistleblower will face criminal charges and probably be prosecuted. The waiver of the immunity seems to be a *vacuum* as it will not protect whistleblowers when they need it the most, namely at the time they take the necessary information to report. As aforementioned, whistleblowers should respect these conditions, a task which seems to be quite challenging.[118] Apart from all the other rules they have to abide by, they also have to be careful with their potential criminal liability.[119] Despite the importance of the way in which the information should be collected in order to prevent the criminal immunity of the whistleblower, the explanations of the Directive are laconic, leaving it to the discretion of Member States to better clarify the conditions of protection from criminal liability.

There are some interesting remarks to make upon this point. The whistleblower will not be criminally liable if two conditions are met. Firstly, the whistleblower should give the appropriate amount of information that demonstrate the existence of a breach falling under the scope of the Directive; and secondly, this information should be acquired in a lawful way. For the protection of whistleblowers, it is necessary to check if a self-standing criminal offence has been committed at the moment of acquiring the necessary information.[120] Thus, if whistleblowers fulfil the self-standing criminal offence requirement, the second condition of waiving the criminal liability is not respected. Therefore, whistleblowers will be criminally liable under national laws and will be up to national judges to decide,[121] considering the proportionality and necessity of the act or omission.[122] As a result, the concept of

118 See: <https://www.whistleblower.org/blog/assessment-of-european-union-whistleblower-directive/> accessed on 12 October 2019.

119 Veronika Nad and Naomi Colvin, Whistleblowing in the European Union: a new Directive to protect citizens, democracy and rule of law, blueprint for free speech, 2019, p. 6.

120 Directive, article 21(3).

121 See: <https://crossroads.ideasoneurope.eu/2019/10/13/the-whistleblowers-protection-directive-reinforcing-transparency-and-accountability-at-the-eu-level/> accessed on 19 October 2019.

122 Directive, recital 92.

self-standing criminal offence and the second condition of waiving the criminal liability are interrelated with regards to the act of acquiring the necessary information. In order to be able to waive the criminal liability, the whistleblower should not commit a self-standing criminal offence when acquiring the necessary information and they should take only the necessary amount. Only in that scenario, the whistleblower will not be criminally liable.

5 Concluding Remarks

The aim of this Chapter was to analyse the past, the present and the future of whistleblowers' legislation in the EU. Despite the obscure past of whistleblowers at the EU level, the advent of the Directive on the protection of persons reporting breaches of Union law marks a new era for the legal protection of whistleblowers in the EU. The path for adopting this Directive was rocky but the European Parliament had a significant role to play to achieve the desired EU legislation. In addition, the different scandals that agitated the European community succeeded in reopening the discussion around the legal status of whistleblowers and what can the EU do, or should do, for them.

In the very early stages of the EU (what was known as European Communities), the whistleblower was not regulated and thus, not effectively protected. This became apparent in the 90s, as well with the case of Paul van Buitenen, and the whistleblower was still a controversial figure. An air of change came when the Treaty of Lisbon entered into force, the European Parliament took more powers, and whistleblowers started to become known as an international concept. As the title of this Chapter demonstrates, whistleblowers in the EU went from obscurity to limelight. The adoption of the Directive sealed the deal for a better regulation of whistleblowing at the EU.

Despite the importance of the Directive and its positive aspects, there are major points of uncertainty and complexity, related to criminal law, that may create obstacles for future whistleblowers. As it was analysed, the issue of the legal bases, where criminal law was not chosen as a legal basis, the concept of the self-standing criminal offence as well as the criminal immunity for whistleblowers may be hurdling points in need of better guidance or explanation. The transposition period and the choices that the Member States will do becomes crucial for the aforementioned points.

To sum up, the Directive constitutes a cornerstone for the protection of whistleblowers at the EU level. Despite some ambiguous points, the Directive is the first EU legal act on this issue, offering the necessary guidelines on the question of whistleblowing. It provides a common definition of whistleblower as well as it clarifies the process towards blowing the whistle. Furthermore, it imposes certain obligation on public and private actors in relation to the organisation of reporting procedure and adopts a protection scheme ranging from civil to criminal law. Finally, the Directive becomes an important step towards a change of culture in relation to whistleblowers, probably leading to a more positive image of them in the near future.[123]

123 Robert G. Vaughn, The successes and failures of whistleblower laws (EE Publishing, 2012) 255.

A Decade of Fast-Track Whistleblowing Legislation: The Quest for Effective Protection of Whistleblowers in Greece

Anna Damaskou and Antonios Baltas

1 The Significance of Culture in Enacting and Implementing Whistleblowing Legislation Effectively

Prevention and early detection: these are the most effective ways to combat crime. Especially corruption cases, which are notoriously secret, may never come to light unless they are reported by people who discover them, for example, in the course of their work. Scandals originating from both the public and the private sectors – with the two sectors often intersecting – remain in the dark for a long period of time, although they are often widely known to a number of non-criminally involved persons. However, in many of those cases, none of those persons decides to break his/her silence and report these illegal acts to the competent authorities or to the general public, even when the law stipulates such an obligation.

The cause of this almost casual failure to report wrongdoing is that it usually carries a heavy cost for the person who actually reports – the so-called "whistleblower". These persons, the whistleblowers, are exposed to significant risks, such as loss of employment, involvement in legal disputes or even facing threats against life. Namely, whistleblowers can avert harm, protect human rights, safeguard lives and financial interests, but all this comes with grave personal sacrifice. This is why whistleblowing is a mere right – it cannot be a legal obligation.

What, however, if the law encouraged such persons to break their silence, by protecting them from retaliation or even reward them for stepping forward against corruption? This was the question posed by Transparency International-Greece to the Greek audience and competent authorities back in 2013, when the country was being tormented by a number of serious scandals in both the public and private sectors, without having a dedicated whistleblowing legal framework in place.

Admittedly, the economic and financial crisis that the country was experiencing at the time, partly as a result of long-lasting economic mismanagement and weak institutions, was per se a convincing argument of why the country should eliminate corruption, but convincing that whistleblowing was

 | DOI:10.1163/9789004459816_004

a sine-qua-non tool towards the achievement of this target was not an initiative without controversy and resistance from competent authorities and the general public. It was obvious that there could be no hope for the enactment of dedicated whistleblowing, if the negative culture and perceptions regarding whistleblowing were not changed first.

Why would this task face any difficulties in a country whose philosophical background included inter alia the concise thinking of Plato, teaching that *"the biggest and first of all evil is those who are unfair to remain unpunished"*[1] and of ancient orator Lykourgos, proclaiming that *"neither the laws or judges can bring any results, unless someone reports the wrongdoers"*[2] and whose legal framework included provisions obliging people to report wrongdoing coming to their attention ever since the times of the Byzantium (Justinianian legislation)?

The dowry was all there, but in Greece the path for whistleblowers is still sown with thorns. Despite the dedicated – still far from effective – whistleblowing legislation enacted in 2014, whistleblowers in Greece still resemble "martyrs" rather than heroes. In the lines to follow, the history of how the country enacted overnight, with a fast-track process, dedicated whistleblowing legislation shall be presented, together with the still ongoing quest for effective remedies.

2 The State of Corruption and Whistleblower Protection in an EU Member State Lacking Dedicated Whistleblowing Legislation

2.1 *Legislation Aiming at the Protection of Whistleblowers before the Enactment of Dedicated Whistleblowing Legislation: A Scattershot Landscape*

Since the emergence of the economic and financial crisis, Greece, usually found near the bottom of the CPI among EU Member States, has been slowly but steadily improving its score and global position in Transparency International's Corruption Perception Index,[3] as the country is implementing an ambitious National Anti-Corruption Plan,[4] throughout the crisis years, so as to, inter alia, tackle widespread mismanagement and lack of accountability, which were the prevailing patterns in the public sector for many decades.

1 Plato (427–347 BC), *Gorgias*.
2 Lykurgus (800–730 BC), *Against Leocrates*.
3 https://www.transparency.org/en/cpi/2020/index/grc.
4 https://aead.gr/publications/esskd.

A number of such scandals of the pre-crisis era shall be presented below. While the scandals were evolving, no dedicated whistleblowing legislation was in place. What was in place were scattered provisions – most of them still in force with the exact same wording, as presented below, which serve similar purposes by offering protection to informants and witnesses.

In more detail, the legal framework in Greece for the protection of whistleblowers before the enactment of dedicated whistleblowing legislation was the following:[5]

- *Article 40 of the Greek Code of Criminal Procedure* contains the provision that even private citizens are obliged, under specific circumstances provided by the law, to report to the Prosecutor or to any other competent official any illegal action which is prosecuted ex officio, when it comes to their attention. The provision does not specify any penalties for its breach. It is also not accompanied by any provisions to protect those who report in accordance with this reporting obligation.
- *Article 252 of the Criminal Code* provides[6] the offence of violation of official secrecy for civil servants who disclosed information, known solely because of civil service, or a document entrusted or accessible to them. The offence was punishable with imprisonment for acts committed with the intent to benefit personally or to damage the state or another. The Article 252 offence applies only to civil servants and to third parties who, being aware of the source and origin of the information and the documents, used them with the intent to benefit personally or to damage the state or another. However, there was an exception (introduced in 2010) to the offence for third parties who disclose necessary information or documents in the interest of informing the public. The exception to criminal liability for disclosure is applicable only to "third parties" and not to civil servants. The exception to liability could potentially extend to citizens or journalists. The exception concerned information and documents related to official public service and not to business of the private sector. However, this notable exception has

5 See relatedly: Transparency International-Greece, *Providing an Alternative to Silence: Towards Greater Protection and Support for Whistleblowers in the EU – Country Report Greece*, 2013: https://www.transparency.gr/wp-content/uploads/2013/11/WHISTLEBLOWERS_ENGLISH_LOW.pdf, OECD, *Whistleblower Protection in the Private Sector: Developing the Legal Framework*, 2018: http://www.oecd.org/corruption/anti-bribery/OECD-Greece-Whistleblower-Protection-Legislative-Proposal-ENG.pdf.

6 The provision has been amended recently.

been abolished after the enactment of the current Criminal Code (enacted with Law 4619/2019).[7]

- Similarly, the breach of professional confidentiality by clergymen, lawyers notaries, doctors, midwives, nurses, pharmacists and other professionals who, due to their profession or their qualifications, are entrusted with confidential information remains unpunished, when the professional aimed to the fulfillment of his/her duties or to securing a legal interest or justified public interest that could not be secured otherwise, in accordance with *Article 371 of the Criminal Code*. Article 371 does not extend to employees other than those usually entrusted with confidential information of people because of their profession or capacity. The object and purpose of Article 371 is to criminalize violation of professional confidentiality, except in cases where a justifiable and substantial legal interest is at stake. As such, it does not provide for protection of potential whistleblowers.
- Like many other jurisdictions, also in Greece those criminally involved persons who contributed substantially in the prosecution of acts of corruption in the civil service, could benefit from suspension of their own prosecution, lower penalties or suspension of the enforcement of the penalties imposed on them, by virtue of former *Article 263B of the Criminal Code*.[8] The Article established four categories of immunity or mitigated sanctions depending on the degree of culpability and status of the reporting person, as well as the status of the accused person:
  i) implicated private persons who reported wrongdoing before the commencement of an investigation;
  ii) implicated private persons who collaborated with law enforcement authorities while the investigation was ongoing;
  iii) implicated civil servants who collaborated with law enforcement authorities while the investigation was ongoing; and
  iv) main civil servant perpetrators who collaborated with law enforcement authorities while the investigation was ongoing.

  More specifically, a private individual who committed or participated in active bribery of a civil servant, bribery of a judge or bribery in the private sector and voluntarily reported to the competent authorities before any investigation commences would not be prosecuted for his/her involvement

7 The repercussions of the abolition of the exception have not been decided by case-law, which was in any case reluctant to refer to it, opting usually to use the constitutional freedoms of information and expressions to resolve issues stemming from journalistic investigations.

8 Already Article 263A of the current Greek Criminal Code (enacted with Law 4619/2019). The new text is not significantly different than the one described here.

in the alleged acts. On the other hand, if the investigations were ongoing and the private individual made a substantial contribution to the discovery of participation of a public official in the corrupt acts, s/he would be punishable by a reduced penalty. At the Prosecutor's request, the Judicial Council might suspend the prosecution and the competent court might also suspend the enforcement of the penalty, if the allegations were proved to be true. Similarly, if the reporting person was a civil servant who participated in a corrupt act and during the investigations made a substantial contribution to the discovery of a public official who was the main perpetrator of the corrupt acts, s/he would be punishable by a penalty reduced to the extent of the first subparagraph of Article 44 (2) of the Criminal Code. At the Prosecutor's request, the judicial council might suspend the prosecution and the competent court might also suspend the enforcement of the penalty, if the allegations were proved to be true. If however, the reporting person was the main perpetrator s/he would be eligible for immunity or mitigated sanctions, only if the following two conditions were met:

i) the accused person held a considerably higher rank than the reporting person

ii) the reporting person transferred to the State all assets they personally and illegally obtained, directly or indirectly through the aforementioned illegal acts.

The main focus of former Article 263B of the former Criminal Code (already article 263A of the current Criminal Code) was to provide for immunities and mitigated sanctions to reporting persons in the civil service who had participated in the corrupt act. Article 263B provided therefore, incentives for implicated persons to come forward and report their collaborators, in return for immunities and mitigated sanctions for criminal prosecution.

- *Article 15, paragraph 2 of Law 3849/2010* also confers protection rights (transfer to another post) to public officials who report crimes of other public officials committed during their service, while witnesses of the crimes of foundation of and participation in a criminal organization and their family members shall be afforded adequate protection, in accordance with Article 9 of Law 2928/2001 on the protection of witnesses. This provision introduced for the first time a comprehensive framework of protective measures for the main witnesses who assist with uncovering relevant criminal activities. The list of measures ranges from extrajudicial protection, starting with police protection and audio and video surveillance, in order to ensure that witnesses and their relatives remain physically unharmed, to relocation within and outside of the country, including the possibility of transferring a civil servant to another unit; to anonymity of the witness in the testimony report, in order to ensure the proper balance of interests as a person may not be condemned only on the basis of an anonymous testimony. The protective regime is granted by Ministerial Decision, upon a proposal by the Public Prosecutor, who must specify the measures requested. The special protective regime is only granted with the consent of the person concerned and the specific measures taken must not limit their personal freedom unduly and beyond what is strictly necessary under the circumstances of the case. Protective measures may be removed, when the protected person requests in writing or when they do not cooperate effectively with the authorities.

2.2 *Indicative Cases of Major Corruption before the Enactment of Dedicated Whistleblowing Legislation*

Around 2013, when the research of Transparency International Greece on the need for enactment of dedicated whistleblowing legislation was published and when the aforementioned legal framework was in place, a number of grave scandals tormented the country and were, thus, reported in the publication in name.[9] Among the most notorious were indicatively the ones mentioned below.

2.2.1 The Ferrostaal Submarines Scandal[10]

In 2000, the then Greek Government, following the decision of the Government Council for Foreign Affairs and Defense, proceeded to order new submarines, choosing to buy from the German company Ferrostaal a new type, for which there was neither a prototype nor a model. Nevertheless, the then Government agreed to buy the first out of the chain of production, on which tests and trials were conducted. It was named "Papanikolis" and was later found to be tilting.

At the end of 2010, the then Government, which came from the same political party as the Government of 2000, signed a revision of the 2000 contract. According to the new agreement, the Greek Government received the "Papanikolis" submarine with a 5-year delay, resigned from the claim of

9 This section is based on the report of Transparency International-Greece, *Providing an Alternative to Silence: Towards Greater Protection and Support for Whistleblowers in the EU – Country Report Greece*, 2013: https://www.transparency.gr/wp-content/uploads/2013/11/WHISTLEBLOWERS_ENGLISH_LOW.pdf.

10 https://sites.tufts.edu/corruptarmsdeals/the-greek-submarine-scandal/.
https://thepressproject.gr/greece-sues-german-arms-manufacturer-over-faulty-submarines/.
https://www.wsj.com/articles/SB10001424052748703636404575352991108208712.

financial penalties of hundreds of millions euro for the delayed delivery of the submarines, consented to the payment of all fines imposed by the European Union and committed to impose almost zero financial penalties for any further delays in the delivery of new submarines.

In a publication by the German magazine "Der Spiegel" reference is made to suspicious payments for the sale of the submarines. As the magazine indicates, *"at the end of October 2010, investigation had not yet identified which politicians and military personnel in Greece, Portugal and South Africa had been bribed"*. However, it underlines that *"the distribution of bribes is not doubted by those charged with the investigation of the case"*.[11]

The case of the Greek submarines was part of a broader investigation on the German company, which was making "non-transparent" payments and was paying bribes abroad. The investigation related to some of the biggest projects of the company along different business sectors in many countries. In the case-file prepared by the Public Prosecutor in Munich there was a reference for non-transparent payments made by Ferrostaal to a so-called secret "prayer circle" – not all of them criminally involved. This cycle appeared to consist of persons of great influence, lobbyists and consultants with strong connections.

The investigation report issued by the Greek Financial and Economic Crime Unit (SDOE) recorded one of the biggest scandals of the past decades, in which over 70 persons appeared to be involved, starting with the then Minister of Defense to consecutive General Armaments Directors, members of the Administration of Skaramanga Shipyards and members of the committees responsible for conducting and monitoring the contracts in question.

The German Justice, by way of a summary procedure, acquitted everyone involved in Germany and in Greece and closed the file by imposing a mere fine of 177 million euro. The Greek Justice imposed criminal penalties on the offenders.

The case has been tried at first instance. The Court of Appeals convicted 20 out of 27 persons. The convictions have been suspended for as long as the appeals of the convicted persons are pending.[12]

---

11 https://www.dw.com/el/%CE%BA%CF%89%CE%B4%CE%B9%CE%BA%CF%8C%CF%82-%CE%BA%CF%8D%CE%BA%CE%BB%CE%BF%CF%82-%CF%80%CF%81%CE%BF%CF%83%CE%B5%CF%85%CF%87%CE%AE%CF%82/a-6430237.

12 https://www.ert.gr/eidiseis/ellada/kinonia/poines-eos-kai-20-chronia-gia-tis-promitheies-ton-germanikon-ypovrychion/, https://www.cnn.gr/ellada/story/163034/ypothesi-ypovryxion-ypsiles-eggyiseis-stoys-katigoroymenoys-gia-na-min-pane-fylaki.

2.2.2 The Social Security Service (IKA) Scandal[13]

Several employees of the social security service (IKA) in the local branch of Kallithea-Athens, one of the largest branches of the social security service in the country, were accused of massive fraud. The employees of the branch were investigated for issuing false certificates, making undue payments and providing undue benefits in kind. The Financial Police proceeded to the arrests of a number of employees. The fraud resulted to a financial damage against for IKA exceeding 12 million euros.

Some of the insured persons who collaborated with the "gang" allegedly admitted to the police that: *"A long time ago, we received a phone call from employees of the IKA branch of Kallithea, who asked us if we wanted to receive a respectable amount of money every month, if we wanted to collect a pretty good allowance. They suggested that we appear as hospitalised patients or ask for other medical services. Then, they would issue the relevant certificates and would enter the relevant data in our health records."* Meanwhile, it was revealed that many other employees of the IKA branch and insured persons who did not benefit in any way from the illegal scheme were aware of the ongoing scheme.

The persons accused for this case have been convicted for computer related fraud, forgery of documents, false statement by public employees and money laundering.[14] The convictions are final, by virtue of a decision of the Supreme Court of Greece for civil and penal cases (Areios Pagos).[15]

2.2.3 The Vodafone Scandal[16]

The phone tapping scandal that occurred during 2004–2005 was also one of the biggest scandals during the past decades in Greece. It involved illegal phone tapping of important public figures.

---

13 https://www.iefimerida.gr/news/41134/eklevan-ekatommyria-apo-ika-kai-estisan-fagopoti-me-syggeneis-kai-filoys http://www.tovima.gr/society/article/?aid=448190. http://www.tovima.gr/society/article/?aid=447465. http://www.tovima.gr/society/article/?aid=447813.

14 https://www.in.gr/2018/06/21/greece/fylakisi-apo-14-eos-27-eti-gia-tis-proin-ypallilous-tou-ika-kallitheas/.

15 http://www.areiospagos.gr/nomologia/apofaseis_DISPLAY.asp?cd=JPIFDE1GR642Q7KMQEHJ2AE4HULFAJ&apof=1166_2019&info=%D0%CF%C9%CD%C9%CA%C5%D3%20-%20%20%D3%D4.

16 https://www.protothema.gr/greece/article/798909/poioi-autoktonisan-ton-kosta-tsalikidi/. https://www.news247.gr/politiki/ypoklopes-kata-karamanli-to-schedio-pythia-o-ths-13-oi-rosoi-kai-i-asimenia-drachmi.6461776.html. https://www.vice.com/el/article/mbkdq3/mia-aytoktonia-poy-htan-dolofonia-h-istoria-twn-ellhnikwn-ypoklopwn-kai-o-tsalikidhs.

The illegal phone tapping was uncovered on March 4, 2005, after a routine check conducted by Vodafone in its software. The Government was informed on March 10, 2005 and revealed the fact to the public on February 2, 2006. It was discovered that, through special software that was installed in the company, about 100 phones were monitored using prepaid "mobile shadow phones", which recorded the conversations. After a two-year judicial investigation that did not yield results, in August 2008, the case was closed. Two years later, in 2010, the case was reopened with the emergence of new evidence that suggested involvement of the US Embassy in an espionage case.

The death of Konstantinos Tsalikidis, a member of Vodafone staff was linked with the case. Tsalikidis, who was responsible for developing the company's network, was found dead on March 9, 2005, a day before the authorities were informed of the existence of the malicious software. His death was initially marked as suicide, a scenario supported by the first judicial report. However, the case was reopened in 2010, as new evidence revealed close connection between his death and the case of the illegal wiretapping and gave grounds to support the possibility of him being murdered.

Evidence showed that high-level executives of Vodafone Greece had been formally informed from Ericsson from about the existence of a system that allowed interception in the software that Vodafone had acquired from Ericsson. The then Vice President and CEO of Vodafone claimed that he had not been informed about this system. The investigation also revealed that five employees of Vodafone had electronic access to the digital center.

Tsalikidis had also expressed great concern to his fiancée about something going wrong in the company. He did not mention anything specific on wiretapping or illegal activity, but he said something bad was happening that, if it was to be made public, it would cause disaster. He had also told his fiancée, in the last days of his life, that him leaving the company was "a matter of life and death."

Until today, the people responsible for these illegal actions have not been traced and no political responsibility has been attributed to any of the two Governments in power during the unfolding of the scandal. Vodafone, on the other hand, denied any involvement in the case.

However, a relevant court decision ruled that *"Vodafone did not exercise due diligence* [...] *and did not report the issue to the competent Public Prosecutor and the competent Hellenic Authority for Communication Security and Privacy. On the contrary, and especially on March 8, 2005, the company disabled the malicious*

https://tvxs.gr/news/ellada/sto-fos-ta-aporrita-arxeia-snooynten-gia-skandalo-ton-ellinikon-ypoklopon.

software, an act that resulted in the loss of critical data for the identification of the perpetrators, since this way they were given the opportunity to be informed that the software has been detected and thus cover their tracks."

3 Can Corruption Be De-rooted without Dedicated Whistleblowing Legislation?

An in-depth reading of the aforementioned scandals that were brought to light at that time, reveals the below similarities and differences between the three cases:

- All of the above cases constitute scandals against the public interest.
- Financial benefit was not always the motive (see, for example, the Vodafone scandal). Consequently, the implications of these scandals were not necessarily of economic nature.
- The cases refer both to the public and the private sector, while in many cases these sectors cross (see, for example, the Vodafone scandal).
- All of the above corruption cases remained in the dark for a significant period of time.
- It was revealed that all of these cases had been known, for a significant period of time, to a wide circle of not criminally involved persons.
- None of those scandals came to light because one of the not criminally involved persons was who knew decided to break his/her silence and report these crimes to the appropriate authorities or to the media.

However, during the period in which these scandals were evolving, Greek law contained provisions on the obligation of every citizen to report to the competent authorities any offence coming to his/her attention.[17] How can it, thus, be ensured that a potential whistleblower shall speak up?

Relevant studies have observed that:[18]

- Employees become whistleblowers, when they feel that the financial standing of their employer is solid.
- Employees become whistleblowers, when they themselves feel financially secure.
- Senior executives tend to become whistleblowers with greater frequency.
- Employees who are members of the relevant labor union tend to become whistleblowers with greater frequency.

---

17 Article 40 of the Penal Procedure Code.

18 Ethics Resource Center, *Inside the Mind of a Whistleblower – a Supplement Report of the 2011 National Business Ethics Survey*, 2012.

- Employees become whistleblowers, when they feel they can be protected from retaliation.
- The more support and social acceptance someone enjoys at a personal, social or professional level the more possible it is to become a whistleblower.
- Most whistleblowers state that they would give up their anonymity, in order to provide information to someone they know and trust.
- Whistleblowers who reported a wrongdoing through external channels, i.e. not to the competent person/body within their employer, claim that they did this because they believed that the moral culture within their employer was questionable.
- Most whistleblowers stated that they are not interested in financial reward. However, persons with financial problems stated that would be motivated to report wrongdoing, if they were such incentives.

The underlying theme of all the above observations is that of security, be it financial or emotional, as each disclosure the disclosure he/she automatically shifts the whistleblower to a sphere of risk ranging from the questioning of their motives to social isolation, job loss, physical harm or even death. A clear, firm and effective legislative framework which at a minimum provides measures for the protection of whistleblowers against retaliation, adequate mechanisms to ensure that disclosures are properly handled and thoroughly investigated is directly linked with the dilemma of whether whistleblowing is the right decision.

4 "… And Then There Was Light": The Enactment of Dedicated Whistleblowing Legislation in Greece

In 2014, Greece took action, so as to comply with its legal obligations emanating from its participation in the 1999 CoE Criminal Law Convention[19] (ratified in 2007) and in the 2003 UN Convention against Corruption[20] (ratified in 2008), as well as from the OECD Working Group on Bribery's Phase 2 and Phase 3 recommendations to Greece on the implementation of the 1997 OECD Anti-Bribery Convention (the 1997 OECD Anti-Bribery Convention was ratified by Greece in 1998),[21] and introduced the notion of whistleblowing into its national legislation.

In more detail:

19 Article 22.

20 Article 33.

21 https://www.oecd.org/daf/anti-bribery/Greecephase3reportEN.pdf.

Article 45B was added in the Greek Code of Criminal Procedure,[22] providing that, in cases related to a number crimes relating to the bribery of certain public officials, it is possible for a person to be characterized as a "witness of public interest", following the approval of the Deputy Prosecutor of the Supreme Court, by an act of the competent Anti-Corruption Public Prosecutor, if that person, without being involved in any way in the said acts and without any intention for personal benefit, contributes substantially with the information he/she provides to the law enforcement authorities in the disclosure and prosecution of the said acts. The aforementioned act of the Prosecutor may be revoked in the same way and at any stage of the criminal proceedings, if the Prosecutor decides that the reasons which led to the issuance of the act do not exist anymore. If a lawsuit has been filed against the witness of public interest for the crimes of perjury, false accusation, defamation or violation of official secrecy, or for personal data violations, the Prosecutor in charge of the criminal prosecution, before any other action, informs the Deputy Prosecutor of the Supreme Court. If the Deputy Prosecutor of the Supreme Court decides after being briefed, as above, that the criminal prosecution of the aforementioned crimes is not necessary for the protection of the public interest, may order the Prosecutor in charge of the criminal prosecution to abstain from the criminal prosecution for the said acts. The protection measures offered to the witness of public interest are the same as those offered to the witnesses of the crimes of foundation of and participation in a criminal organization

After Article 45B was passed, the *Civil Service Code was amended* to ensure that a public official who has been declared as a witness public interest under Article 45B of the Code of Criminal Procedure shall not be excluded from promotions or become subject to any disciplinary proceedings or punished, or dismissed or otherwise subjected to any direct or indirect discrimination, in particular in matters promotion, transfer or placement, during the investigation of the case,[23] and that no disciplinary measures shall be undertaken because of their whistleblowing.[24] If such an official is subject to disciplinary measures, the disciplining body must demonstrate that the measures are not retaliatory in nature i.e. the

22 After the entry into force of the current Greek Code of Criminal Procedure (enacted with Law 4620/2019), Article 45B is now Article 47 of the new Code of Criminal Procedure.

23 Articles 26 paragraph 4 of the Civil Service Code.

24 Article 110 paragraph 6 the Civil Service Code.

burden of proof is reversed.[25] Officials who report corruption may also be transferred upon their request.[26] Finally, the anonymity of officials who contribute substantially to revealing corruption is guaranteed during preliminary investigations and in certain circumstances thereafter.[27]

A concise critique of the Greek legal framework on whistleblowing as it currently stands could not possibly omit the following points:[28]

- The authority(-ies) to which the whistleblower should report the wrongdoing is not specified.
- The range of crimes for which protection is offered to whistleblowers is very limited: the objective scope of the former Article 45B of the Greek Criminal Procedure Code (already Article 47) is only the crime of bribery in the public sector – not even in the private sector. Most notably, not even money laundering of the proceeds of the covered offences is covered. An effective whistleblowing framework would require the inclusion of all forms of crimes.
- The requirement that the person reports without any intention for personal benefit is both an unjustified, as there is no reason why a legitimate personal benefit (such as e.g. a promotion) should not be sought, and difficult to establish. This good faith requirement should be restricted only to a "best knowledge and belief" requirement.
- In principle, the law protects not only employees but every person (i.e. even journalists and activists) who provides information to the competent prosecuting authorities.
- The protection offered to public interest witnesses under former Article 45B (already Article 47) is extremely limited. If a complaint is lodged against them for the offences of perjury, false accusation, defamation or violation of official secrecy and the Deputy Public Prosecutor of the Supreme Court deems that the prosecution of the public interest witness does not serve the public interest, s/he may order the competent prosecutor to abstain from

25 Article 139 paragraph 4 of the Civil Service Code.

26 Article 73 paragraph 6 of the Civil Service Code.

27 Article 125 of the Civil Service Code.

28 Panagopoulou-Koutnatzi Fereniki, *The Institution of the Witness of Public Interest* (*whistleblowing*)*: an Ethico-Constitutional Consideration*, 2016; Stylianidou Maria, *Protection of Employees as Whistleblowers in the Public Sector: Whistleblowers in International Organizations and in States of Europe*, 2017; OECD, *Whistleblower Protection in the Private Sector: Developing the Legal Framework*: http://www.oecd.org/corruption/anti-bribery/OECD-Greece-Whistleblower-Protection-Legislative-Proposal-ENG.pdf.

prosecution. The protection therefore is not automatic, but it is at the discretion of the Prosecutor.

- But even if the prosecutor decides to abstain, the public interest witness is not totally protected from such complaints, because the protection concerns criminal prosecution and not claims for civil damages.
- What is more, Article 45B does not provide any protection against discriminatory or disciplinary retaliation, such as dismissal from employment, demotion, punitive transfer or workplace harassment, but only the protection measures of Law 2928/2001 (see above).
- The requirement that protection is afforded only if the disclosure leads to prosecution of the offences makes things even more complicated; the mere disclosure of true crimes does not suffice.
- The non-provision of any financial or other benefits is another compromising instance of the law, which in fact does not offer any encouragement to potential whistleblowers to speak up and report wrongdoing.
- Finally, the right of the whistleblowers to receive information on the development and outcome of their reporting is not introduced.

5 The Novartis Scandal in Greece: A Stress-Test for the Greek Whistleblowing Legislation and Culture

The Novartis case in Greece refers to an investigation by the Greek and US judicial and regulatory authorities into the alleged bribery of government officials and doctors of the Greek public and private sectors by the multinational pharmaceutical company Novartis, for promoting its business interests. The investigation into the Novartis case was initially initiated by the US Securities and Exchange Commission (SEC) and the US Department of Justice, following the aforementioned allegations. In parallel with the judicial development of the case in the USA, an investigation was initiated in 2018 by the Greek justice, based on the testimonies of three witnesses of public interest (i.e. whistleblowers) against inter alia ten government officials of the period 2006–2015, including two former Prime Ministers and a number of Ministers. The implicated government officials categorically denied all charges against them and filed multiple lawsuits against the three witnesses of public interest.

In more detail, in August 2016, initially two, and then three, Greek citizens, former high-level employees of Novartis in Greece, testified to the US authorities that the company uses unlawful methods to improve its position in the Greek pharmaceutical market for a number of years, to the detriment of other pharmaceutical companies. The witnesses submitted documents indicating, among other things, payments by the company to doctors of the public and private sectors. At the end of December 2018, the Anti-Corruption Prosecutor prosecuted one of the key witnesses for passive bribery. As a result of the prosecution, the witness of public interest was transformed into an accused person.

Attempts by the government officials to "unmask" the identities of the whistleblowers were intense. They referred to the "fabricated testimonies of anonymous people", "musketeer witnesses", "scoundrels" and "slanderers". Those government officials were more or less the same persons that, in 2014, in their capacity as MPs, voted the law which introduced the notion of whistleblowers in the Greek legal system for the first time (Article 45B of the Greek Code of Criminal Procedure).

In June 2020,[29] the subsidiary Novartis Hellas agreed to pay the amount of $ 225 million in an out-of-court settlement with the US authorities, acknowledging that from 2012 to 2015 the company proceeded with unlawful benefits to doctors of the Greek public and private sectors. In light of this event, the question whether the witnesses of public interest should receive in Greece any protection status at all has been raised, as they may have made the disclosure with the expectation to receive a percentage of the financial fines imposed in a foreign jurisdiction and, thus, they made the disclosure with the intention of personal benefit, which is contrary to the Greek law.

6 The Efficiency of Whistleblowers' Protection in Greece in View of the Transposition of the EU Directive on the Protection of Whistleblowers

Having reviewed the national legislative framework for the protection of whistleblowers currently in force, it is of value to focus on the how whistleblower protection actually works in practice. To this end, assessing the efficiency of the operation of internal and external reporting channels, as well as of the protective measures against retaliation allows the drawing of conclusions particularly useful in in view of the upcoming transposition into the Greek legal order of the EU Directive on the protection of whistleblowers.

---

29 https://www.sec.gov/news/press-release/2020-144. https://www.justice.gov/opa/pr/novartis-hellas-saci-and-alcon-pte-ltd-agree-pay-over-233-million-combined-resolve-criminal.

6.1 *Internal Reporting Channels*

By virtue of the relevant legislation and of the Presidential Decrees providing of the organizational charts of the Ministries, internal control units have been established in the Ministries,[30] with responsibility to, *inter alia*, receive complaints. However, no procedure with the characteristics of the "internal reporting channel" described in the EU Directive on the protection of whistleblowers[31] (confidentiality, independence and obligation to follow-up on the report of the whistleblowers) seems to be provided for by the relevant legislation. Internal control units are established not only in *stricto sensu* public sector, but also in legal entities of public law and in local government, in addition to the private sector. However, no general obligation for internal reporting channels is in force for the private sector, except for specific exceptions as provided in law,[32] without this meaning that there are no initiatives by private sector entities to establish internal reporting channels.

An illustrative example of such an exception is found in par. 2 of Article 39 of Law 4443/2016, according to which employers participating in activities that fall under the regulatory framework governing the provision of financial services, should establish appropriate internal procedures, so that their employees can report violations of EU Regulation 596/2014.[33] The Regulation in name is important for the implementation of the EU Directive on the protection of whistleblowers, since the Regulation falls within the scope of the Directive. So, in fact, this Regulation acts as a precursor to the protection of whistleblowers at the EU level.

6.2 *External Reporting Channels*

A significant number of public entities manage external reporting channels for receiving complaints on various issues. An interesting and important record of the numerous entities with competence to receive complaints about corruption is presented in the "Report on the Implementation of Corruption Complaints Management Mechanisms in Greece",[34] which was prepared, in 2018, by the

30 Article 39 of Law 4622/2019.

31 Directive (EU) 2019/1937 of the European Parliament and of the Council of 23 October 2019 on the protection of persons who report breaches of Union law.

32 International Labor Organization, Law and Practices on Protecting Whistleblowers in the Public and Financial Services Sectors, 2019, pp. 25–26.

33 Regulation (EU) No 596/2014 of the European Parliament and of the Council of 16 April 2014 on market abuse (market abuse regulation) and repealing Directive 2003/6/EC of the European Parliament and of the Council and Commission Directives 2003/124/EC, 2003/125/EC and 2004/72/EC.

34 https://www.oecd.org/governance/ethics/6.1.1-mapping-corruption-complaints-mechanisms-greeceel.pdf.

Organization on Economic Cooperation and Development (OECD), as part of the program "Greece-OECD: Provision of Technical Assistance for the Fight against Corruption".[35] In this report, which was published before the establishment of the National Transparency Authority, in 2019, which merged a number of public investigative bodies, the fragmentation of the external reporting channels is recorded. This report states[36] that the existence of many bodies is not necessarily negative, provided that there is coordination in the management of complaints and the existence of specific criteria, which – obviously correctly – was found not to be the case. Nevertheless, an external reporting channel very close to the description of the EU Directive on the protection of whistleblowers is provided in Article 39 par. 1 of Law 4443/2016, pursuant to Article 32 of EU Regulation 596/2014, in conjunction with Decision 1/798/12.10.2017 of the Hellenic Capital Market Commission, incorporating the EU Implementing Directive 2015/2392.[37] Moreover, by virtue of Article 67 of Law 4706/2020, regarding the violations of EU Regulation 1129/2017[38] and of the relevant legislation, the Hellenic Capital Market Commission should establish a secure channel of communication with the complainants of the specific violations, while employers who undertake activities that are subject to the specific regulations in the field of provision financial services have an identical obligation. Such provisions are expected to substantially contribute to the proper incorporation of the EU Directive on the protection of whistleblowers.

6.3 *Protective Measures against Retaliation*

The protection of employees against retaliation is provided in Greek law for all employees, in accordance with Article 5 of Law 2957/2001, pursuant to Article 9 of the Council of Europe Civil Law Convention against Corruption. According to this provision of the Greek law, any form of penalty against an employee or public official, on the basis that (s)he reported acts of corruption to competent persons or authorities is prohibited, unless (s)he acted in bad faith or without reasonable suspicion and the complaint proved to be unfounded." The

35 The receipt of technical aid was provided in Article 3 par. c (5.3) of Law 4336/2015.

36 https://www.oecd.org/governance/ethics/6.1.1-mapping-corruption-complaints-mechanisms-greeceel.pdf, p. 18.

37 Commission Implementing Directive (EU) 2015/2392 of 17 December 2015 on Regulation (EU) No 596/2014 of the European Parliament and of the Council as regards reporting to competent authorities of actual or potential infringements of that Regulation.

38 Regulation (EU) 2017/1129 of the European Parliament and of the Council of 14 June 2017 on the prospectus to be published when securities are offered to the public or admitted to trading on a regulated market, and repealing Directive 2003/71/EC.

provision, which has not been accompanied by any additional measures, does not seem to have impacted legal practice.

Nevertheless, the much older Decision 470/1977 of the Supreme Court has impacted legal practice. In the context of the case in name, an employee, who had made complaints of administrative misconduct of a private-law legal entity, initially before the General Assembly of the legal entity and then through the press, was protected from unlawful dismissal. The Supreme Court endorsed the judgments of the lower courts, which had invoked the general clause of Article 281 of the Civil Code on the prohibition of abuse of rights.[39]

Although the use of a general clause does not meet modern needs, nevertheless, this important legal precedent can contribute to the harmonious integration of new legal notions into our legal order. Furthermore, as already described above, more specialized provisions for protection against retaliation have been enacted after the entry into force of Law 4254/2014, which concern only employees of public-law legal entities,[40] provided that the person has been characterized as a "witness of public interest" (whistleblower),[41] which refers exclusively to crimes of bribery.

Finally, fragmented provisions can be found in other legal instruments, such as in Article 46 par. 4 of Law 3850/2010 regarding safety and health at work,[42] and in Article 7b of Law 3610/2007, as in force after the entry into force of Law 3842/2010, which promises compensation to taxpayers who reveal cases of bribery of tax officials. In order for the latter provision to be implemented, the issuance of a ministerial decision was required, which has not been issued yet[43] and, in any case, did not have any serious impact in practice. However,

39 D. Goulas, "The Dismissal of an Employee due to the Publication of Irregularities of the Company", article in Greek in the Greek journal Labor Law Review ("Epitheorisi Ergatikou Dikaiou"), 2017, pp. 582–584, who, commenting on the decision, identifies an argumentative proximity with the whistleblowers protection approach of the case law of the European Court of Human Rights.

40 See, indicatively, the report prepared in the Greece-OECD Project: Technical Support on Anti-Corruption, *Whistleblower Protection in the Private Sector: Developing the Legal Framework*, p. 11, where the shortcomings of the current regulation are further explained, in accordance with the Phase 3bis Evaluation Report of the OECD Working Group on Bribery (2015): https://www.oecd.org/daf/anti-bribery/Greece-Phase-3bis-Report-EN.pdf.

41 Article 45b of the prior version of the Code of Criminal Procedure and already Article 47 of the current Code of Criminal Procedure.

42 D. Goulas, "The Dismissal of an Employee due to the Publication of Irregularities of the Company", article in Greek in the Greek journal Labor Law Review ("Epitheorisi Ergatikou Dikaiou"), 2017, p. 560 and footnote 22.

43 Official statement of the then Deputy Minister of Finance in the Plenary Session of the Parliament: https://www.minfin.gr/content/-/asset_publisher/NqgEa4zG2NyO/content/omilia-tes-yphypourgouoikonomikon-k-papanatsiou-sten-olomeleia-tes-boules-kata

the provisions of Articles 6 and 7 of Law 3610/2007 are referred to in the case law of the Supreme Court, in cases of passive bribery of tax officials, with the latter invoking them as an argument in their defense.[44]

To conclude this brief presentation, it is obvious that the protection of whistleblowers is clearly not effective in the Greek legal order and should be strengthened, without simply modifying existing provisions. The same conclusion can be drawn with regard to the operation of internal and external channels, both in the public and private sectors.

7 The Transpositon of the EU Directive on the Protection of Whistleblowers into the Greek Legal Order[45]

EU Member States have until December 2021 to transpose the Directive. This is an opportunity for all EU countries to bring their national legal framework on whistleblower protection in line with international standards and best practices. However, as the Directive has admittedly a number of loopholes and weaknesses,[46] the issue is not only to uphold the undertakings of the Directive, but also to reinforce them, in line with the preamble of the Directive, which urges Member States to act in the spirit of the Directive and not strictly in its letter, so as to offer a high level of protection for whistleblowers reporting breaches of law, whether EU or national law.

Thus, when transposing the Directive into national legislation, Member States should take the opportunity to close loopholes and strengthen weaknesses of the Directive, ensuring comprehensive and effective protection to all whistleblowers. Such an endeavor shall, *inter alia*, require the sincere cooperation of all co-competent authorities within a Member State, the "broad-minded" transposition of the Directive, so as to benefit from its spirit, together with awareness-raising and public engagement throughout this process. In the lines to follow, Greece shall serve as a case-study for context-specific recommendations as to process which could be followed at the national level.

-te-syzetese-kai-psephise-tou-n-s-ensomatose-sten-ellenikenomothesia-t?inheritRedirect=false.

44 Decisions of the Supreme Court 610/2015 and 470/2016.

45 See relatedly: Transparency International-Greece, *Effective Transposition of the EU Directive on the Protection of Whistleblowers: Analysis And Suggestions by International Transparency-Greece*, 2020.

46 See indicatively: Transparency International, *Building on the EU Directive for Whistleblower Protection: Analysis And Recommendations*, 2019: https://images.transparencycdn.org/images/2019_EU_whistleblowing_EN.pdf.

7.1 *Co-competent Public Authorities*

As all EU Member States, Greece is also obliged to transpose the EU Directive on the protection of whistleblowers by 17.12.2021. This is a complex task, which will *de facto* require the cooperation of a number of co-competent ministries, such as:

- the Ministry of Justice, which is responsible for judicial protection measures and the introduction of grounds for the non-imposition of penalties,
- the Ministry of Development and Investments, which supervises and enacts legislation for legal entities under private law,
- the Ministry of Interior, which is responsible for the introduction of new procedures in all legal entities under public law and local government, and
- the Ministry of Finance, which supervises sectors for which the operation of whistleblowing mechanisms is already obligatory.

In parallel, Independent Authorities will obviously have a central role in shaping the new framework. These include, *inter alia*, the National Transparency Authority, which should in fact have oversight and/or operate as a central external reporting channel, the Hellenic Capital Market Commission, which has already established the most advanced system of internal and external complaint channels regarding capital-market violations, while it has also taken initiatives to improve corporate governance. Namely, the recent enactment of Law 4706/2020, which significantly strengthens corporate governance, should be strengthened by the proper transposition of the EU Directive on the protection of whistleblowers.

It goes without saying that the issue is also of interest to the Single Independent Public Procurement Authority, as public procurement is a key area for strengthening integrity, as well as to the Hellenic Data Protection Authority and the Hellenic Financial Intelligence Unit (FIU).

Finally, the involvement of the Ombudsman is equally important, given that the institution in name has a clear picture of citizen-state relations and the authority to receive and process complaints and reports related to violations of law and of human rights.

7.2 *Stengthening the Provisions of the EU Directive on the Protection of Whistleblowers*

Enactment of a single national legal framework for the protection of whistleblowers, which inter alia shall:

- Protect persons who report any violation of law, as well as any threat or harm to the public interest.
- Provide internal and external reporting channels which shall guarantee confidentiality, efficiency, impartiality and independence in receiving and

managing complaints, always with respecting to the institutional framework and available resources.

- Extend protection measures to:
  a) civil society organizations assisting whistleblowers,
  b) persons suspected – even wrongly – of being whistleblowers, and
  c) persons intending to report.
- Clearly impose the burden of proof on the person who took the detrimental measures against the person who reported a wrongdoing.
- Not require complainants to meet additional conditions for obtaining protection in legal proceedings.
- Provide comprehensive monetary and non-monetary compensation measures to whistleblowers.
- Provide for dissuasive penalties for public and private entities that do not operate internal reporting channels in accordance with the provisions of the Directive.
- Provide for the acceptance of anonymous reports.

7.3 *Benefits from the Fast and "Broad-Minded" Transposition of the EU Directive on the Protection of Whistleblowers*

The transposition of the EU Directive on the protection of whistleblowers with a timeline shorter that the deadline provided by the Directive and also with a scope widen than the one provided by the Directive would be a very serious indication that Greece attaches great importance to strengthening transparency and promoting integrity. This indication could also have a measurable impact on public opinion and the international image of the country. Besides, it must be taken into account that the protection of whistleblowers will be of concern to Council of Europe's Group of States against Corruption (GRECO), in the framework of its 5th Evaluation Round.

For these reasons, the mobilization of all competent public authorities, as well as of the private sector should commence on time. The best way to give the relevant stimulus is the public commitment of the Greek government that the transposition of the Directive – in a way that shall meet in the best possible way the international standards – will take place well in advance before the transposition deadline provided by the Directive. The means to formulate this commitment could be the forthcoming National Action Plan for Open Government.[47] Through such a commitment, a roadmap for the fast and appropriate transposition of the Directive could be implemented.

47 https://www.opengovpartnership.org/members/greece/.

7.4 *The Role of Transparency International-Greece Transposition of the EU Directive on the Protection of Whistleblowers*

Having developed extensive action and international know-how in matters of whistleblower protection,[48] since 2013, Transparency International(-Greece) considers whistleblowing to be the most effective early warning tool for reporting misconduct in the public and private sectors. The transposition of the EU Directive is a first-class opportunity for Greece to keep pace with countries that play a leading role in protecting those who report irregularities and illegalities. Transparency International-Greece has proposed a process of open dialogue and cooperation in the framework of the National Action Plan for Open Government. The bodies responsible for the transposition of the EU Directive and the law-drafting committee, with the support of Transparency International-Greece, as well as of other public and private bodies, can cooperate, in order to transpose the European Directive in a timely manner and with a high level of protection, so that Greece embodies international best practices,[49] filling the gaps of the existing institutional framework, while, at the same time, promoting in the public and private sectors a culture of encouraging corruption reporting. Such a commitment within the Open Government Partnership, which emphasizes the priorities, could be the following:

Immediately after the adoption of the new law, a platform for the provision of information to public and private legal entities shall be created, so as to keep up to date management and employees about the new protection framework. The purpose of such public communication is to provide information on whistleblowing legislation and reporting procedures. Thus, citizens shall not be afraid to speak up about abusive and illegal practices in their workplaces.

Throughout the implementation of such a commitment, Transparency International Greece, in the framework of its long-standing cooperation with organizations throughout Europe, shall support the effort of public and private bodies to comply on time and effectively with the obligation to establish internal reporting channels.

---

48 See indicatively: Transparency International-Greece, *Providing an Alternative to Silence: Towards Greater Protection and Support for Whistleblowers in the EU – Country Report Greece*, 2013: https://www.transparency.gr/wp-content/uploads/2013/11/WHISTLEBLOWERS_ENGLISH_LOW.pdf.

49 A Best Practice Guide for Whistleblowing Legislation. Transparency International – διαθέσιμο εδώ: https://images.transparencycdn.org/images/2018_GuideForWhistleblowingLegislation_EN.pdf.

8 The Significance of Culture in Providing Effective Whistleblowing Protection under the Demands of the New Era

In December 2019, Li Wenliang, a Chinese doctor who worked at Wuhan Central Hospital shared with his colleagues information about the possible outbreak of an illness that resembled SARS (and was eventually assessed to be the novel disease of Covid-19), encouraging them to protect themselves from infection. He was characterized as a whistleblower only later, when his message became publicly known and, as a result, Li Wenliang was summoned to the Public Security Bureau in Wuhan, where he was accused of false statements that disturbed the public order and was asked to revoke the said statements and refrain from repeating them. The doctor, who was in fact one of the first people to recognize the outbreak of Covid-19, returned to work and later contracted the disease from a patient who was not known to be infected. He died from the disease, in February 2020, at the age of 33.

Li Wenliang sounded the alarm on time, but the Chinese authorities opted to silence the whistleblower, instead of flagging the issue to the world. Would Li Wenliang have faced different treatment by public authorities having found himself in a Greek context? The developments of the Novartis case do not guarantee a different development of the story.[50]

Nevertheless, whistleblowing has proven to be a powerful tool in preventing and combating actions that undermine the public interest. In the era of the pandemic, in particular, when decisions are taken under emergency circumstances, often without democratic control for the sake of speediness, whistleblowers can serve the vital task of early warning. Especially in a period of international health crisis, whistleblowers are the safety mechanism in any society, since the public needs to know whatever may have life or death repercussions for them. In such times of crisis and thereafter, when public and private accountability should be maintained and the rights and freedoms of all people should be upheld, whistleblowers should be afforded maximum protection, as their role in detecting irregularities and illegalities is extremely critical, given that justice, transparency, accountability and cooperation are even more vital than ever before.

50 See relatedly: Transparency International, "In Times Like This Transparency Matters More Than Ever: the Need for Transparency and Accountability during the Covid-19 Pandemic Goes Beyond Health Systems", 19.03.2020: https://www.transparency.org/en/news/in-times-like-these-transparency-matters-more-than-ever; Vigjilenca Abazi, "Truth Distancing? Whistleblowing as Remedy to Censorship during COVID-19", in Bioethical Inquiry Journal, May 2020: https://www.ncbi.nlm.nih.gov/pmc/articles/PMC7242766/ Jing-Bao Nie & Carl Elliott, "Humiliating Whistle-Blowers: Li Wenliang, the Response to Covid-19, and the Call for a Decent Society" in Bioethical Inquiry Journal, August 2020: https://www.ncbi.nlm.nih.gov/pmc/articles/PMC7445730/.

Protecting Whistleblowers in Israel: The Gap between the Law and Its Implementation

Noa Yosef

1 Introduction[1]

Whistleblowers expose corruption and other illegal acts before they come to public light. As such, they are society's first line of defence against organisational malpractices and wrongdoings. However, when the prospect of retaliation is high and the level of legal protection is low, potential whistleblowers may find themselves harmed and powerless. Like many countries, Israel has recognised the need to protect whistleblowers from the retaliation they often suffer due to blowing the whistle. On the surface, Israeli whistleblowers have multiple options of protection to choose from, mainly through labour law, criminal law, and a special procedure under the Ombudsman of Israel. However, despite encouraging rhetoric in the laws and some judgments, the road for a whistleblower seeking protection is often exhausting and full of hurdles. This chapter examines the main protective laws Israel offers its whistleblowers and assesses how effective they are in their actual implementation. It concludes that although the letter of the Israeli laws protecting whistleblowers is reasonably comprehensive (though far from perfect), questions about their practical effectiveness remain open. Offering whistleblowers multiple options of legal action can achieve more effective protection, but only as long as those options are put to actual and attentive use.

To address this issue, this work will start by shortly presenting the background to Israel's legal regime – providing the setting within the legal rules offered to Israeli whistleblowers are enacted and applied. The next section discusses the two main laws dealing with the protection of whistleblowers in Israel: [1] The Protection of Employees Law (Exposure of Offences of Unethical Conduct and Improper Administration) 5757–1997 [PEL], [2] The State Comptroller Law, 5718–1958 [SCL]. Theoretically, these laws offer whistleblowers comprehensive protection mechanisms. Mechanisms that encompass criminal and civil domains, and offer procedures both inside and outside the court system. However, as will be shown, some procedures offered by these laws are scarcely used, and others present hurdles to the whistleblower seeking

1 All translations in this article are by the author unless stated otherwise.

 | DOI:10.1163/9789004459816_005

protection, creating a gap between the written law and its realisation. The third section extends the analysis to the civil-labour option of the PEL's and SCL's procedure. The use of labour law and the focus on labour relations when protecting whistleblowers is further discussed and developed. This discussion lays the groundwork for the final section, which explores the complementary use of the criminal and labour-civil options offered by Israeli laws. This complementary use offers well-rounded protection that can take advantage of each legal branch's different aims and strengths. Nevertheless, without the actual implementation of all legal options, this protection will remain ineffective.

2 Background

In order to understand the legal position of whistleblowers in Israel, it is important to understand the legal framework within which the whistleblower's protection operates. The Israeli legal system is a mixed jurisdiction system.[2] At its founding, the State of Israel could be considered a common-law jurisdiction.[3] Since then, however, Israel's legal regime has been influenced by and infused with civil law traditions.[4]

For whistleblowers, the two main relevant legal channels are labour and criminal. Israeli Labour laws reflect the mixture of jurisdiction.[5] In 1969, a separate labour courts system was established[6] that dealt with both collective labour relations and private employment disputes,[7] as is traditionally prevalent in Continental Europe.[8] The influence of English common law has mainly manifested in the Israeli criminal justice system in Israel (though there is no jury)[9]

2 For elaboration *see*, Aharon Barak, *Some Reflections on the Israeli Legal System and Its Judiciary*, 6(1) *Electronic Journal Of Comparative Law* (2002) <http://www.ejcl.org/61/art61-1.html>; Tamar Gidron & Stephen Goldstein, *Israel*, in *Mixed Jurisdictions Worldwide: The Third Legal Family* 577, 578 (Vernon Valentine Palmer ed., 2 ed. 2012).

3 According to Gidron & Goldstein.

4 *Id.*, at 577–578.

5 *Id.*

6 *Report of the Commission to Review of Labour Courts* 31–33 (Jerusalem 2006).

7 Labour Courts Law, 5729–1969, Art. 24.

8 Manfred Weiss, Re-inventing labour law?, in *The idea of labour law* 43, 43 (Guy Davidov and Brian Langille ed., 2011).

9 *See*, Douglas Evan Beloof & Dana Pugach, *Comparing Modern Victims' Rights in Israel and America: Israeli Victims' Rights Need Remedy*, 8(1) *International Perspectives in Victimology* 11, 22–23 (2014); Gidron & Goldstein, *supra* note 2, at 579.

and in private employment disputes in labour courts.[10] However, like most Israeli laws, private employment disputes were introduced and assimilated with the concept of "good faith," which derives from classic continental law.[11]

Israeli law offers two main incentives to whistleblowers – protection and recognition. Protection is offered through two main channels, which both deal with whistleblowers who have suffered retaliation, and derive from employment relations and organisational memberships. The first is the PEL, which encompasses both criminal and civil-labour procedures. The second is the SCL, that creates a dedicated procedure managed by the Ombudsman. These laws are the main focus of the next chapter. Regarding recognition, it is important to mention the Encouragement of Public Morality in Public Service Law, 1992 [EPMSL]. According to this law, a public employee who makes an initial complaint that is according to procedure, in good faith, and determined valid will get a Certificate of Findings with the examination results. This law is meant to encourage public employees to devote efforts and attention to prevent corruption.[12] Additionally, the law authorises the President to award whistleblowers a Certificate of Appreciation for their actions. However, the first presidential certifications were given only in 2015, 23 years after the law was enacted, and have been awarded only once more since then.[13] Unlike the PEL and SCL, the EPMSL does not offer protective measures for whistleblowers that suffered retaliation. However, like the PEL and SCL, the EPMSL demonstrate the gap between these laws written word and their implementation, as will be discussed next.

3 Israel's Main Laws for Protecting Whistleblowers

3.1 *Protection of Employees Law*

The PEL aims to protect employees who submitted, or helped submit, a complaint against their employer or an employee of their employer.[14] The labour court interprets this law as having a dual purpose:[1] protecting the employee who blows the whistle and [2] encouraging other employees to expose

10 *Id.*, at 587.

11 *Id.*

12 Explanatory notes for the Draft Bill to enact the Encouragement of Public Morality in Public Service Law, 1992, H.H., proposal 2114, p. 221.

13 *See*, the Government Services and Information Website <https://www.gov.il/he/Departments/General/certificate_of_appreciation>.

14 Protection of Employees law, Art. 2.

corruption.[15] For that purpose, the law forbids an employer, or supervisor acting on behalf of the employer, to retaliate against such employees.[16] Under Israeli law, retaliation means unjust harm to the employee's "work matters" including working conditions, promotions, professional training, dismissal or severance pay, employee benefits, and payments concerning retirement from work.[17] The courts also define various harms to "work matters," such as job transfers, salary reduction, work deprivation,[18] slander, and false complaints made against the employee-whistleblower.[19] Violations of the PEL are in the jurisdiction of the Labour court.[20] Employees from both the public[21] and private sectors are protected under the PEL. However, while protections in the private sector are given only when the whistleblower exposes an unlawful act, the PEL's coverage in the public sector extends to reports about unethical conduct and administration.[22]

The PEL distinguishes retaliation in two ways: as a [1] criminal offence punishable with an arrest of up to three years or a fine of up to 75,300 NIS; [2] civil wrong eligible for [A] compensation, including up to 500,000 NIS exemplary compensation if circumstances are especially severe; and [B] any warrants needed, such as warrants for reinstatement or prohibition of dismissal, if the court finds that compensation alone is unjust. When issuing such warrants, the court must consider their effect on the relations within the workplace, and

15 National Labour Court 2561/09 Rotem v. State of Israel Ministry of Finance, para 17 (published in Nevo, Sep. 9, 2007).

16 Protection of Employees law, Art. 2a(a).

17 Protection of Employees law, Art. 1.

18 *See e.g.*, National Labour Court 17365-11-11 Suissa v. Yehud Municipality, para 31, 70 (published in Nevo, May 3, 2014).

19 *See e.g.*, National Labour Court 502/05 Gerti v. State of Israel Ministry of The Interior, para 29 (published in Nevo, Jul. 25, 2006); National Labour Court 20567-11-11 Hazut v. Israel Railways Ltd., para 93 (published in Nevo, Jun. 04, 2013).

20 Protection of Employees law, Art. 3(a).

21 Under this law, public sector means: [1] Government ministries and state institutions. [2] Local municipalities and corporations under the municipalities control. [3] Corporations established by law and government companies, as defined in the Government Companies Act, 1975. [4] corporations whose business is governed or controlled by a specific law to the kind of business it administers. [5] A recognized educational institution, as defined in the Compulsory Education Law, 1949. [6] Higher education institutions, as defined by the Council for Higher Education Law, 1958. [7] HMOs, as defined in the State Health Insurance Law, 1994. [8] Workers' unions and employers' unions, as well as corporations under their control. [9] The World Zionist Organization. [10] The Jewish Agency for Israel. [11] The Jewish National Fund. [12] Keren Hayesod. [13] Any enterprise, institution, foundation, or other body that the government participates in under its management. *See*, Protection of Employees law, the schedule to the law.

22 Protection of Employees law, Art. 4(2).

the possibility of harm that might be caused to other employees.[23] Protection warrants may be issued only for whistleblowers working for public employers, or for private employers employing more than 25 employees.[24] Disobeying court rulings can be met with all enforcement powers given to the court, such as contempt of court charges.

To be recognised as a whistleblower and thus be entitled to protection under the PEL, the Plaintiff-whistleblower must meet several criteria. First, there must be a causal-link between the retaliatory action and the initial complaint. The disclosure of wrongdoing needs only to be considered; it does not need to be the sole reason behind the harm towards the whistleblower's work matters.[25] Since the law was amended in 2008,[26] the burden of proof falls first on the employee, who must show that [1] she was mistreated by the employer or by a supervisor on the employer's behalf ;[2] that there was no reason for the mistreatment in her actions or behaviours; [3] the initial complaint was submitted within a year since the mistreatment. Once these are shown, the burden is transferred to the employer to show that there was no retaliation.[27] Even after the 2008 amendment, failing to prove the causal-link is still the main reason whistleblowers' lawsuits are rejected.[28]

Under the PEL, whistleblower recognition also requires the initial complaint to be submitted in good faith to an approved authority that is eligible to receive or investigate the complaint.[29] The meaning of good faith under this law is obscure. The courts interpret this concept broadly, and not always consistently. In the Gerti case, the court linked the requirement of good faith with the requirement of a legitimate motive, specifically excluding employees who filed the initial complaint out of revenge or disgruntlement.[30] In the Abergel case, however, the court states that the motive for filing the initial complaint should not be considered when examining the plaintiff's good faith.[31] According to the Abergel case, good faith needs to be examined by the circumstances:

---

23 Protection of Employees law, Art. 3(a).

24 Protection of Employees law, Art. 3(c).

25 Rotem, *supra* note 15, para 21.

26 Explanatory notes for the Draft Bill to Amend the Protection of Employees (Exposure of Offences of Unethical Conduct and Improper Administration) Law, (burden of proof), 2001 H.H., proposal 3039, p. 6.

27 Protection of Employees law, Art. 3a.

28 Eliad Shraga, *Whistle Blowers* 191–194 (2017). (Hebrew).

29 Protection of Employees law, Art. 4(1), 4(3).

30 Gerti, *supra* note 19, at para 14.

31 National Labour Court 41182-02-12 Abergel v. Joint Israel, para 85 (published in Nevo, Feb. 20, 2017). Even though the Abergel case pursues the Gerti case and therefore is the obligating precedent, later ruling still cite the Gerti case or follow its principles. *See e.g.*,

did the employee take reasonable steps to determine whether the complaint was genuine? Was the complaint formed, fashioned, and filled in the manner that would cause the least possible harm, given the circumstances?[32] When examining good faith, the court also favours internal reporting.[33] Additionally, according to the Abergel case, whether or not the whistleblower's behaviour was in good faith needs to be examined not only before the whistleblowing act but after as well.[34] This requirement makes it even harder for whistleblowers to gain protection. The scholar and activist Eliad Shraga claims that for its over-comprehensiveness, ambiguity, and scrutiny of whistleblower motivations, the concept of 'good faith' has become an almost insurmountable obstacle in the way of whistleblowers seeking protection.[35] Is should be noted that a report that is not in good faith exposes the reporter to compensation.[36]

The limitation period for the PEL is 12 months, counted from the act of wrongdoing – i.e., the retaliation. Exceeding the limit prevents one from suing for the retaliation under the PEL, but it does not prevent suing for the retaliation on other grounds, such as tort or contractual. This short limitation period has been criticised by some legislators as impairing the law's deterrent capacity and preventing harmed employees from suing.[37]

Gaining recognition and protection under the PEL civil-labour option is not easy. Gilboa et al. conducted a multiple case-law analysis and found that 82% of the plaintiffs who sought protection under the PEL were denied.[38] When a remedy was provided, it was typically monetary compensation.[39] The researchers divided the arguments made by the courts for rejecting recognition and protection into four groups: [A] the employee or the complaint violated

---

Tel-Aviv District Labour Court 2316-03-15 Eisenberg-Bachar v. Clalit Health Services, para 35–36 (published in Nevo, Mar. 27, 2020).

32 Abergel, *supra* note 31, at para 66–67.

33 *See e.g.*, Gerti, *supra* note 19, at para 14; Shraga, *supra* note 28, at 183.

34 Abergel, *supra* note 31, at para 85.

35 Shraga, *supra* note 28, at 489–490.

36 Protection of Employees law, Art. 3(c).

37 Amendment's proposal of The Protection of Employees (Exposure of Offences of Unethical Conduct and Improper Administration) (Amendment – the extension of the period of limitation whistleblower lawsuit against his employer), 2018.

38 In their study, Gilboa Levy and Rosman examined 34 decisions, including 25 lawsuits in the district court and nine appeals in the national court. The district court affirmed six of the claims, of which one employee returned to work. The rest were granted compensation. Nineteen claims were dismissed. All appeals were dismissed; in seven of them, the plaintiffs were required to compensate the employer. *See*, Meir Gilboa, Ina Levy and Nir Rosman, *Has the Gate Been Broken? The Case Characteristics of Claims Regarding the Protection of the Gate Alerts*, 6–7 (2011) (Hebrew).

39 *Id.*, at 3.

workplace harmony and undermined labour relations; [B] the bad relationships ensued not because of the complaint, but rather the whistleblower's personal flaws, sometimes even perceived lack of integrity; [C] the court diminishing the reported behaviour; [D] the defects exposed by the whistleblower had already been corrected.[40] The first three arguments transfer the focus from the employer's acts to the employee's behaviour – leading to rulings that there were no causal-link or good faith. The latter assumes that an organisation that fixes the reported malfunctions has no interest in harassing the whistleblower. Yet, in practice various actors in the organisation may maintain resentment and anger toward the whistleblower.[41] Furthermore, an organisation can treat the wrongdoing since its exposure, and still retaliate against the whistleblower to set an example and discourage further exposures.[42]

Even when the employee is recognised as a whistleblower, she will probably receive unsatisfying remedies. Monetary compensation is first among court discretion,[43] but the compensation awarded by the court is usually low.[44] There has been limited use of exemplary compensation. To my knowledge, the court has not granted exemplary compensation to its fullest,[45] and usually incorporates it into other types of compensation, such as loss of earnings.[46] Scholars and activists in the field of whistleblowers often note the remedy of reinstatement as preferable, although the court rarely awards it.[47] The examination of the implications of a warrant on labour relations and the effect on other employees within the organisation often leads to the denial of such remedies,

40 *Id.*, at 8–10.

41 *Id.*, at 10.

42 *See*, Janet P. Near & Marcia P. Miceli, *Effective Whistle-Blowing*, 20(3) *Acad. Manag. Rev.* 679, 688 (1995); Marcia A. Parmerlee, Janet P. Near & Tamila C. Jensen, *Correlates of Whistleblowers' Perceptions of Organizational Retaliation* 27 *Adm. Sci. Q.* 17, 19–20(1982).

43 Protection of Employees law, Art. 3(a)(2); Shraga, *supra* note 28, at 545.

44 *See e.g.*, Navot's claim that higher compensation is needed in some whistleblowing cases, Doron Navot, *Whistleblowers: What Does Their Suffering Reveal About the Abuse of Power in the Organization and the Structure of Power in Society?* 21 *IDC Law Review* 229, 259 (2018). (Hebrew).

45 According to a search conducted in Nevo (an Israeli computerized legal database). The search was conducted on May 25, 2020 searching for rulings referencing article 3(a)(1) of the PEL which grants the labour court the power to award exemplary compensation of 500,000 NIS.

46 *See e.g.*, Hazut, *supra* note 19, para 87.

47 *See e.g.*, Shraga, *supra* note 28, at 134, 587; Adler and Shemer-Begas note that not only is reinstatement or relocation in the workplace are the preferred remedy, but that this is also the stance of the labour court in the Gerti case, *see*, Steve Adler and Reut Shemer-Begas, *Whistleblowers in Labour Law*, *Strasberg-Cohen Book* 583, 600 (Aaron Barak, Yitzhak Zamir, Avner Cohen, Moran Saburai, Elad Afari Ed., 2017). (Hebrew).

leaving whistleblowers without a fitting job.[48] Thus, the heavy burden of the exposure's consequence is imposed on the whistleblower. Even scholars who oppose reinstatement in the same workplace agree that, to encourage and protect whistleblowing, there is a need to provide, when necessary, another equal or better workplace.[49]

When the criminal procedure of the PEL is used, the labour court follows the general criminal procedure's law.[50] The office responsible for receiving, investigating, and forwarding complaints to the prosecution is the Regulation and Enforcement Administration [REA] within the Ministry of Labour, Social Affairs, and Social Services. The criminal prohibition of retaliation was enacted in 2008. Since then, as of June 2019, only 42 complaints were received in the REA. An investigation was opened for 13 of these complaints, from which two had indictments. One was closed with a contingent liability arrangement, and the other ended with a verdict.[51] These numbers suggest that, despite the letter of the law, PEL in practice rarely results in criminal proceedings. For comparison, between 2008 and 2019, when only two criminal cases were brought to the labour court, over 110 decisions and rulings were given in labour courts under civil-labour proceedings.[52] Moreover, regarding criminal enforcement of other labour laws by the REA, between 2015–2018, an investigation file was opened for 550 cases,[53] for which 348 indictments were filed, and only 173 cases received sentence.[54] The PEL's criminal procedure is slim compared to the civil and other criminal procedures initiated by the REA.

48 Gilboa Levy and Rosman, *supra* note 38, at 10–11.

49 For this suggestion regarding public employees *see*, Navot, *supra* note 44, at 259.

50 Labour Courts Law, Art. 24(b).

51 Information provided by the REA on Aug. 12, 2019, Pursuant to a request made by the writer according to the Freedom of Information Law, 5758–1998.

52 The number is a result of a search conducted in Nevo (an Israeli computerized legal database). The search was conducted on Apr. 26, 2020 searching for rulings and decisions that mention the PEL as a ground for the lawsuit. The count was according to cases – meaning decisions and rulings under the same case-number or sided were counted as one case. Of course, these results do not take into account lawsuits that did not end with a ruling, so it is safe to assume that a higher number of lawsuits have been filed in practice.

53 Cases were open based on complaints the REA received by employees and on proactive enforcement actions taken by the REA. *See*, *Regulation and Enforcement Administration – Activity Summary for 2018*, p. 9. <https://employment.molsa.gov.il/About/Units/RegularizationAndEnforcement/AnnualReports/sikum2018.pdf>.

54 *Regulation and Enforcement Administration – Activity Summary for 2015*, p. 9; *Regulation and Enforcement Administration – Activity Summary for 2016*, p. 9; *Regulation and Enforcement Administration – Activity Summary for 2017*, p. 11; *Regulation and Enforcement Administration – Activity Summary for 2018*, p. 11. All summaries are available in <https://employment.molsa.gov.il/About/Units/RegularizationAndEnforcement/Pages/AnnualReports.aspx>.

3.2 *State Comptroller Law*

The SCL allows the state comptroller, in his role as the Ombudsman of Israel, to investigate whistleblowers' complaints about retaliation. Generally, the Ombudsman is not allowed to examine the complaints of employees, but the legislature makes exceptions for two groups whose protection is deemed particularly important: whistleblowers and internal auditors.[55] When the Ombudsman finds a complaint about retaliation justified, she can provide a variety of remedies, such as monetary compensation, temporary or permanent reinstatement, and prevention of action.[56] Unlike the PEL, the Ombudsman cannot award both types of remedies – it is either a mandatory injunction or monetary compensation.[57] Another important distinction between the two laws is that the SCL does not forbid retaliation, but offers an inquiry procedure when a complaint is made. Hence, it is protective and not preventive in nature.[58] The SCL, however, does demand that employers regulated under this law inform their employees about the option to contact the Ombudsman if they feel retaliated against due to blowing the whistle.[59] This channel is open to a limited sector of employees: employees in institutions under the supervision and inspection of the State Comptroller as detailed in the law.[60] Company officers (such as directors) are not eligible for the protection of this law.

Like the PEL, the SCL regulates employees who expose or help expose corruption or severe violations of legislation or proper administration. The initial report must be filed following the proper procedure and with good faith. 'Proper procedure' means: [A] reporting perceived corruption via internal organisation mechanisms, or [B] reporting externally to the state comptroller or enforcement agencies. Nevertheless, in the rare cases where there is justification for diverting from the proper procedures, the Ombudsman has discretion and may still assist the whistleblower.[61] 'Good faith' means that the

55 *Ombudsman Annual Report 44 for the year 2017*, Office of the State Comptroller and the Ombudsman, p. 169, (2018).

56 State Comptroller Law, 5718–1958, Art. 45(c)(a).

57 State Comptroller Law, Art. 43c(b); Shraga, *supra* note 28, at 540.

58 *Id.*, 163.

59 State Comptroller Law, Art. 45f.

60 Controlled institutions are: government offices; enterprises or institutions of the State; persons or bodies that holds, not under a contract, the property of the State or manages it or controls it on behalf of the State; local municipalities; government company, as defined in the Government Companies Act, 1975 as well as enterprise, institution, foundation or other body that the government participates in its management; any person, enterprise, institution, foundation or other body that is subject to review by law, by decision of the Knesset or by agreement between them and the government; *See* State Comptroller Law, Art. 9.

61 State Comptroller Law, Art. 45a–45b; *Ombudsman Annual Report* 44, *supra* note 55, at 170.

employee reasonably believes the facts and charges she reported are true.[62] The motivation for the whistleblowing act is not part of this examination.[63] To gain protection, the whistleblower also needs to show a causal-link between the retaliation and the complaint, meaning that the exposure significantly impacted the acts of the employer. After the employee has shown the above, the employer must prove that its actions were fair, and motivated by legitimate and objective reasons.[64] Most employees who turn to the Ombudsman for recognition and protection as whistleblowers fail to receive it.[65]

The complaint investigation process may be lengthy. First, all parties whom the Ombudsman believes can shed light on the subject will be contacted. After that, preliminary findings and conclusions are formulated and forwarded for response to the parties who might be harmed. If needed, a supplementary investigation takes place. Only then does the Ombudsman make her final decision.[66]

To offer the whistleblower and her family more holistic assistance, the Ombudsman may assign a social worker to assist the whistleblower and her family during, and even after, the complaint inquiry process. Despite favouring monetary compensation, the Ombudsman also recognises the significant harm of losing a job. To correct this, the Ombudsman office works with the employment bureau, the civil service commissioner, the chief of police, and the witness protection program, aiming to help the whistleblower find new employment.[67] These alternative channels are of high importance where mandatory injunctions are given sparingly.[68] There are no similar services in the Labour Court.

It should be noted that the Ombudsman will not investigate a complaint when the issue is pending in a court or tribunal,[69] meaning the employee must choose between them. Additionally, while the proceeding before the court has a built-in traditional right to appeal to a higher court,[70] the Ombudsman's decision cannot be appealed. In unique cases, the Attorney General may request the Ombudsman to reconsider her decision. In the case of a State-employee

62 Chaim Kalchheim, *White Corruption in Israel*, in *The Struggle Against Corruption: A Comparative Study* 53, 64–65 (Roberta Ann Johnson Ed., 2004).

63 *State Comptroller Opinion – Protection of Whistleblowers, Office of the State Comptroller*, p. 10 (2007).

64 *Ombudsman Annual Report 44*, *supra* note 55, at 170.

65 Shraga, *supra* note 28, at 543–544.

66 *Id.*, at 171.

67 *Ombudsman Annual Report 44*, *supra* note 55, at 167.

68 Regarding the low number of protection warrants given by the ombudsman, *see*, Shraga, *supra* note 28, at 543.

69 State Comptroller Law, Art. 38(5).

70 Basic Law: The Judiciary, 1984, S. H. 1110, Art. 17.

complaint, the Civil Service Commissioner may also request the Ombudsman to reconsider the decision, and if the complainant is not a State-employee, the head of the audited body may also so request.[71]

Supplementary to the SCL is the Civil Service Code. This code prohibits the retaliation and harassment of whistleblowers, thus adding a preventive dimension to the SCL. These regulations also incorporate the PEL and regulate procedural issues concerning retaliation complaints.[72]

A main problem with this channel is its feeble enforcement power. A warrant infringement constitutes a disciplinary violation,[73] and the infringer may be criminally liable. However, as noted in an amendment proposal for the SCL law that seeks to establish a mechanism for monitoring orders issued by the Ombudsman:

> In practice, many times the relevant officials who are in charge of criminal and disciplinary enforcement are not at all aware of the breach of the order or do not use the tools available to them to enforce it.[74]

In case of infringement, the state comptroller may consider filing a complaint with the police or the Attorney General, to examine whether criminal proceedings are appropriate. Although violations of orders are common,[75] filing complaints is still a rare and unusual step.[76]

---

71 State Comptroller Law, Art. 45h.

72 The Civil Service Code, Chapter 43.5.

73 State Comptroller Law, Art. 45h. Disciplinary judgment is a legal procedure for public employees (in the broad sense) and other professionals obligated by law to have a disciplinary system (such as lawyers and doctors). Disciplinary judgment is separated from criminal law. The first deals with the enforcement of ethical obligations, while the latter deals with general criminal norms. *See*, Menachem (Mario) Klein and Aviad Igra, *A New Model for Disciplinary Punishment of Criminal Offenses Involving Moral Turpitude*, 20 *Colman Law Review*, 145, 146–147 (2014). (Hebrew).

74 Explanatory notes for the State Comptroller Bill (Amendment – Implementation of Protection Orders for whistleblowers), 2015 – amendments were not enacted.

75 As stated by Amichai Shai, the State Comptroller's Special Advisor, in a hearing of the Knesset's State Audit Committee. See 'For the first time, in a precedential step: The State Comptroller will file a complaint with the police for a breach of a protection order given to an internal auditor in a local authority,' *The Knesset news – the Knesset website* (Jun. 10 2018). <https://main.knesset.gov.il/News/PressReleases/pages/press10.01.18ll.aspx> (Hebrew).

76 In 2017 the Ombudsman appealed to the Attorney General to examine the possibility to initiate criminal proceedings against officials in Sderot municipality who violated a protective order. *See Ombudsman Annual Report 44*, *supra* note 55, at 173. In 2018 for the

The Ombudsman has final say in each case; thus, the process and results are heavily dependent and influenced by the Ombudsman herself. This leaves the process prone to bias and to personal and political interventions, since the Ombudsman is appointed and supervised by the Knesset (the Israeli Legislative Power). Furthermore, the Ombudsman's discretion is vast, and she is subject to a scanty judicial review only if a fundamental flaw was made in the decision.[77]

4 Criticism against the Protection of Employees Law and State Comptroller Law

Both the PEL and SCL have been the subject of similar criticism, highlighting their main issues and deficiencies. First, as can be seen in the previous part, while both offer powerful protection and remedies, they are also full of hardships for the whistleblower seeking to obtain them. Second, both laws do not have a sufficient deterrent effect on retaliators. When compensation is given, it is usually paid by the employer (the organisation/company/state) and not by the person (or persons) directly responsible for the retaliation.[78] In "Civil Security", the one criminal case which received a sentence, the organisation's owner, who was also its manager, was exonerated. The court ruled that he did not meet the law requirement of 'a supervisor appointed by the employer', since he was not in charge of the working conditions, hiring, or dismissal of employees.[79] The organisation, on the other hand, was found guilty for the retaliation and fined 25000 NIS.[80]

Burdening the organisation and not the actual retaliator not only undermines deterrence, but might even be considered unfair, as highlighted in a

first time, the State Comptroller's Office filed a complaint to the police against a mayor who violated a protective order. *See*, Sachar Ilan, 'Precedent: The State Comptroller filed a complaint with the police against a mayor for violating a whistleblower's protection,' *Calcalist* (Jun. 1, 2018). (Hebrew).

77 On the Ombudsman vast discretion *see* Shraga, *supra* note 28, at 432.

78 *See*, Shraga, *supra* note 28, at 587; Navot, *supra* note 44, at 260; for a rare example where the wrongdoer was charge with part of the compensation because of the severity of his actions *see*, Tel-Aviv District Labour Court 46609-01-11 Shoshani-Gino v. Ramat Hasharon municipality, para 102 (published in Nevo, 20.05.2012).

79 Cr. C. Be'er-Sheva District Labour Court 19352-05-13 State of Israel, Ministry of Economy v. Civil Security S.K. Ltd., para 21–22 (published in Nevo, Feb. 25, 2015).

80 *Id.*, at para 15.

rare statement by a first-tier court in the civil case of Or v. Tel Aviv District Association of Craft and Industry,

> … where the court is convinced that the dismissal was unlawful, the court has two options: one, providing [contract] enforcement, and the other, providing financial compensation. In this case, the remedy of compensation for the dismissal is unjust, and I will explain. The defendant is funded by membership fees paid to her by the employers' sector. Why the compensation's burden, in the number of hundreds of thousands of shekels, should fall on the shoulders of the association members when it is clear that the plaintiff's flawed dismissal process was done by the defendant's heads and at their fault.[81]

Thus, one is left to wonder why this reasoning is not considered relevant when dealing with state or public companies, who are founded by the public that should not be burdened with the compensation due to the retaliators' actions.

The third criticism is that the laws do not advance the design of ex-ante reporting, prevention, and protection mechanisms within the organisation. A partial answer exists in Israel's Companies Law 5759–1999. This law obligates public companies and private companies that have issued bonds in the stock exchange to have an audit committee that creates measures to handle employee complaints about company conduct deficiencies and that provides means to protect such employees.[82] This is a partial mechanism since it does not have a distinct preventive component – i.e., retaliation is not forbidden and punishable. Of course, the law may motivate a committee to publish a Code of Conduct prohibiting retaliation and establishing preventive measures, but it is not obligated to do so. It should be noted that the objective of this law is not the protection of the employee but the improvement of a company's ability to address deficiencies in its business.[83] Furthermore, it excludes a large segment of employees.

A fourth criticism is that "employee" is a narrow status that prevents protection to organisation members that are not formally considered employees. This category includes members like contract workers, freelancers, vendors and outside contractors, who are in a position to gain knowledge about

81 Tel-Aviv District Labour Court 42523-03-12 Or v. Tel-Aviv District Association of Craft and Industry, para 38 (published in Nevo, Oct. 10, 2012).

82 Companies Law 5759-1999, Art. 114, 117(6).

83 Explanatory notes for the Draft Bill to Amend the Companies Law (Amendment 12) (Improving Corporate Governance), 2010, H.H., proposal 496, p. 573.

wrongdoings and corruption and may be vulnerable to harm if they report, thus leaving them unwilling to do so without proper incentive.[84] For example, freelancers and vendors who work with the state for specific projects might be exposed to bid-rigging and avoid reporting it in fear of jeopardising future engagements with the state. Furthermore, neither laws protect police officers, correctional officers, and soldiers, who are not considered employees under Israeli labour laws.[85] Though these groups can sue under different laws in other courts and tribunals,[86] they do not have some of the shortcuts afforded by these whistleblower protection laws, like compensation without proving damages, the PEL's change in the burden of proof, and the acknowledgment these specific laws offer. This criticism is of high importance when thinking of today's labour market, where more employment practices fall outside the traditional employee-employer relation. Thus, modern employment relationships would not get the protection of labour laws in general, nor the protections given to whistleblowers specifically, where "traditional" characteristics of an employee are still needed to be acknowledged as one, leaving the employer the power to manipulate employee's status.[87]

In 2007, the State Comptroller himself made recommendations for a more inclusive PEL. Part of his recommendations suggested including contractor's workers, and employees harmed by colleague retaliation.[88] The law changed soon after, adding the possibility to sue for retaliation committed by a supervisor on behalf of the employer.[89] It is clear that this new wording does not include retaliation from a colleague. When a colleague independently retaliates against the whistleblower, the latter can sue him under tort law and slander – again, without the shortcuts afforded by the specific laws. It is not clear whether the change will be interpreted according to the state

84 For a general criticism regarding labour law and its failure "to respond to changes in employment practices and other changes affecting the labour market ... which in practice means that many workers are left outside the scope of protection (entirely or partially), with case law and legislation ...", *see* Guy Davidov, *Setting labour law's coverage: Between universalism and selectivity*, 34(3) *Oxf. J. Leg. Stud.* 543, 548–549 (2014).

85 State Comptroller Law, Art. 45a; Shraga, *supra* note 28, at 323–328.

86 *See e.g.*, HCJ 6840/01 Palzman v. Chief of Staff, IDF. (3) 121 (2005); AP (Administrative Tel-Aviv) 30939-04-15 Drakts v. State of Israel (published in Nevo, Jul. 14, 2016).

87 For elaboration *See*, Guy Davidov, *Re-matching labour laws with their purpose*, in *The Idea of Labour Law* 179, 182–184 (Guy Davidov and Brian Langille ed., 2011). On the distinction between employees who are characterized by dependency and democratic deficit (subordination), and "workers" who are characterized only by dependency (mostly economically), *see* Guy Davidov, *Who is a Worker?*, 34(1) *Ind. Law J.* 57, 57–58 (2005).

88 *State Comptroller Opinion*, *supra* note 63, at 27–28.

89 Amendment to the Protection of Employees Law (2008).

comptroller's recommendation to protect contract workers when the relevant case is submitted.[90] It should be noted that the Israeli courts use a purposive approach when allocating employment rights so that some rights are given to workers who are not employees.[91] Thus, through the purposive approach, broader protection for non-traditional employees might also be possible without changing the law.[92]

Another similar criticism is that labour laws do not grant protection to whistleblowers external to the organisation. Outsiders like journalists, civil society organisations, and politicians who might be in a position of knowledge, interest, and ability to expose wrongdoings remain unprotected as whistleblowers by labour laws. Whether to consider these populations as whistleblowers is not obvious. While some consider that organisation membership is mandatory for whistleblower acknowledgement,[93] others have broader definitions.[94] Under Israeli law, members of these groups, and organisation outsiders generally, are not considered whistleblowers. However, when needed, they also may find remedy under other areas of law, such as tort law and slander.

At this point I wish to elaborate on the inherent connection labour laws have with whistleblowing. At the base of labour law lies the conception that there is an imbalance in bargaining power between employer and employee, in favour of the employer.[95] Labour law acknowledges the unique relationships

---

90 In the protocols of the Labour, Social Welfare and Health Committee hearings, where they discussed the amendments for the Second and Third voting for law, the discussions regarding the addition of "a supervisor on behalf of the employer" revolved around different types of supervisors within the workplace and not about contract workers. *See*, *Social Welfare and Health Committee protocols* from 20.5.06, 30.6.06. To my knowledge, the relevant discussion has not been made in the Israeli labour court rulings.

91 *See*, Guy Davidov, *A Purposive Approach to Labour Law* 197–221 (2016).

92 On the possible use of purposive approach regarding whistleblowers who are not traditional employees *see*, Shraga, *supra* note 28, at 317–319.

93 *See e.g.*, Janet P. Near & Marcia P. Miceli, *Organizational Dissidence: The Case of Whistle-Blowing*, 4 *J. Bus. Ethics* 1, 2–3 (1985). For elaboration on the favourability of the narrow definition *see* Paul Latimer & A.J. Brown, *Whistleblower Laws: International Best Practice*, 31 U.N.S.W.L.J. 766, 775–776 (2008).

94 *See e.g.*, William De-Maria, *Whistleblowers and organizational protesters: Crossing imaginary borders*, 56(6) *Curr. Sociol.* 865, 866 (2008); for elaboration on the various definitions given to whistleblowers *see*, Nadia Smaili & Paulina Arroyo, *Categorization of whistleblowers using the whistleblowing triangle*, 157(1) *J. Bus. Ethics* 95, 97–98 (2019).

95 Weiss, *supra* note 8, at 43–44; John Howe, *The broad idea of labour law: Industrial policy, labour market regulation and decent work*, in *The Idea of Labour Law* 295, 295 182–184 (Guy Davidov and Brian Langille ed., 2011); Hugh Collins, Gillian Lester, &

constructing the labour market and labour contracts, characterised by personal dependencies, and inherently dealing with human dignity and basic needs.[96] Those characterisations correspond with the whistleblowing act, which is based on power imbalance and stems from the whistleblowers lacking "(...) the power to directly affect changes in organisational practices".[97] The harm caused by retaliation, which usually includes shunning, defamation, and financial damage, penetrates the heart of human dignity, and is possible through power imbalance. An organisational connection is inherent to the process of whistleblowing, and the employment relation is a clear example of such a connection.[98] It is this connection that, in enabling the whistleblower to gain inside information, also establishes the emotional and economic dependencies that make him vulnerable. As explained by Latimer and Brown:

> Members of the public do not usually need legislative protection to report wrongdoing, especially concerning services or matters that affect them personally, because they are not normally subject to the same organisational loyalties and risks of reprisal that affect an organisation's own employees (...) In most jurisdictions, the consequences of unlimited whistleblowing are more negative than positive, diluting the purpose and focus of the legislation, confusing its operation and creating 'floodgate' fears about the potential number of complaints, which have in turn led to attempts to narrow the scope or implementation of the legislation in other areas (such as by limiting the types of wrongdoing that may be reported).[99]

Even under the demand for an organisation or employment connection (with the possibility for a broader definition of what an employee is), the whistleblower can still select multiple procedural options – criminal and civil-labour. These will be elaborated on next.

Virginia Mantouvalou, *Introduction: Does Labour Law Need Philosophical Foundations?*, in *Philosophical Foundations of Labour Law* (Collins, Lester & Mantouvalou Eds. 2018).

96 *Id.*; on the vulnerabilities associated with being an employee, and specifically dependency *see*, Davidov, supra note 91 at 34–52.

97 Terance Miethe & Joyce Rothschild, *Whistleblowing and the control of organizational misconduct*, 64(3) *Sociol. Inq.* 322, 324 (1994).

98 Latimer & Brown, *supra* note 93, at 775–776.

99 *Id.*

5 Criminal Laws and Civil-Labour Laws – Complementary Mechanisms

Criminal and civil-labour laws and procedures aim to address different societal needs and goals, which is reflected in how they handle retaliation specifically. One may consider the different options as complementary mechanisms, offering a more comprehensive legal solution to the retaliated whistleblower's needs.

5.1 *The Criminal Option*

Criminal law and procedure are essential tools in the fight against corruption. Criminal law sets the boundaries between forbidden and permitted behaviours,[100] essentially defining much of what is considered corruption. The use of criminal law to protect whistleblowers seems to be a logical extension of the criminalisation of corruption. Criminal law and procedure have several advantages for whistleblowers. Since the state conducts the criminal trial and it is the state responsibility to investigate and manage the legal proceedings, thus removing the burden of conducting a trial from the whistleblower. Criminal procedure also offers the possibility of compensation (albeit lower), and the opportunity for vindication.[101]

In Israel, the main criminal law provision for protecting whistleblowers is the PEL, meaning the relevant criminal option is under the umbrella of labour law and is in the jurisdiction of the labour court. Nevertheless, it is still a criminal law and falls under criminal law's objectives, principles, rules, and procedures.[102] When thinking of criminal law, and punishment, certain aims come to mind: retribution, deterrence (personal and general), incapacitation, rehabilitation, and (most recently) restoration.[103] However, without proper enforcement, these objectives cannot be fulfilled, and this is the case

100 Andrew Ashworth & Lucia Zedner, *Defending the Criminal Law: Reflections on the Changing Character of Crime, Procedure, and Sanctions*, *Crim Law and Philos* 21, 22 (2008); Boaz Sangero, *Critique of The Israeli Criminal Law* 57 (2020) (Hebrew).

101 Nils Jareborg, *Criminalization as last resort (Ultima Ratio)*, 2 *Ohio St. J. Crim. L.* 521, 530 (2004). On denunciation as one of the criminal law's aims *see*, David Lanham, Bronwyn Bartal, Robert Evans & David Wood, *Criminal Laws In Australia* 4 (2006).

102 Labour Courts Law, Art. 24(b).

103 For elaboration on retribution, deterrence, incapacitation and rehabilitation *see* Michele Cotton, *Back with a Vengeance: The Resilience of Retribution as an Articulated Purpose of Criminal Punishment*, 37 *Am. Crim. L. Rev.* 1313, 1315–1317 (2000); on the restorative goal as part of the restorative approach to criminal law (as oppose to the punitive approach) *see* Hadar Dancig-Rosenberg & Tali Gal, *Restorative Criminal Justice*, 34 *Cardozo L. Rev.* 2313, 2324 (2013).

in Israel.[104] Without enforcement and punishment, there is obviously neither retribution, incapacitation, rehabilitation, nor restoration. Allegedly, the law's mere existence fulfils the objective of deterrence that will prevent the retaliation against whistleblowers. However, for deterrence to take place, there is a need for visible enforcement,[105] since a key element for deterrence is one's subjective assessment of the probability of being caught and punished.[106] This has more effect than the punishment's severity.[107] Implementation and operation of the PEL's criminal option could potentially answer the criticism about the PEL's and SCL's lack of sufficient deterrent effect, and advance other criminal law's objectives.

The same can be said about the possibility of awarding up to 500,000 NIS exemplary compensation – the highest exemplary compensation in the Israeli labour laws. This compensation is part of the civil proceedings, but it has a punitive component that signals the severity the legislature attributes to retaliation against whistleblowers.[108] However, the court has never awarded the full sum,[109] likely reducing its deterrent effect.

The gap between the criminal law's available tools and their actual use undermines even the declarative message, leaving the criminal option of the law as a dead letter.

5.2 *Whistleblowers as Crime Victims*

Since retaliation is an offence, whistleblowers who have been retaliated against are crime victims. As such, they are entitled to some rights under the Israeli Rights of Crime Victims Law.[110] This law differentiates categories of victims, providing more rights to those victimised by more severe offences.[111]

104 *See* above – Protection of Employees Law.

105 Paul H. Robinson, *Does Criminal Law Deter? A Behavioral Science Investigation*, 24(2) *Oxf. J. Leg. Stud.* 173, 173 (2004).

106 *See*, J.L. Miller & Andy B. Anderson, *Updating the Deterrence doctrine*, 77 *J. Crim. L. & Criminology* 418, 421–422 (1986); On the importance of police presence to produce deterrence *see*, Andrew Golub, Bruce D. Johnson, & Angela Taylor, *Quality-of-life policing, Policing* (2003) <https://www.ncbi.nlm.nih.gov/pmc/articles/PMC3889019/>.

107 Miller & Anderson, *supra* note 106, at 438; the certainty of the likelihood of being caught affects the deterrent effect, even when the penalty is less severe *see*, Aaron Chalfin & Justin McCrary, *Criminal deterrence: A review of the literature*, 55(1) *J. Econ. Lit.*, 27 (2017).

108 Protection of Employees law, Art. 3(a)(1); Adler & Shemer-Begas, *supra* note 52, at 595–596.

109 *See*, *supra* note 45.

110 The Rights of Victims of Crime Law, 2001.

111 Beloof & Pugach, *supra* note 9, at 24.

In Israeli law, retaliation is considered a misdemeanour.[112] Consequently, the rights given to whistleblowers in criminal proceedings are at the bottom of the rights scale, granting only rights to: [1] attend the trial and be accompanied by a person of their choice; [2] receive, when asked, certain information and documents, including the right to browse the indictment; [3] submit a victim impact statement regarding the damage and injury caused by the perpetrator, in case of a conviction; [4] receive protection from the defendant and his associates, when possible; [5] be notified, upon request, about stages in the criminal proceeding.[113] Under Israeli law, a violation of rights granted under the Crime Victims' Rights Act neither qualifies the victim to a remedy nor invalidates the criminal proceedings.[114]

These partial rights offer whistleblowers in the criminal proceedings limited control and participation. For example, whistleblowers in the criminal procedure cannot, on their initiative, directly address the court. They cannot state their opinion on what is an appropriate punishment or whether to use a plea bargain.[115] Criminal proceedings are known to be hard and sometimes even harmful to victims, precisely because they mirror the victims' painful experience of the offense.[116] Whistleblowers' experience regarding their actions and the consequential retaliation may have strong psychological effects, including feelings of exclusion[117] and lost control.[118] Criminal proceedings might reproduce those feelings – excluding the whistleblower from the management of the case and giving him limited rights – thus adding to the harmful experience. Furthermore, the remedies available under the criminal proceeding are limited and include compensation of up to 258,000 NIS[119] without reinstatement possibilities.

It seems that, even if the criminal procedure were used, in its current shape, though it might offer deterrence and satisfy the need for vindication and

---

112 Protection of Employees law, Art. 5a.

113 *See*, The Rights of Victims of Crime Law, Art. 3, 6–11, 15, 18; Beloof & Pugach, *supra* note 9, at 24–25.

114 *Id.*, at 27; The Rights of Victims of Crime Law, Art. 21.

115 Edna Arbel, *The Crime-Victim's Status in The Legal Proceedings*, in *Gabriel Bach Book* 189, 211 (2011).

116 Bruce J. Winick, *Therapeutic Jurisprudence Perspectives on Dealing with Victims of Crime*, 33 *Nova L. Rev.* 536, 542 (2009); Jamie Balson, *Therapeutic Jurisprudence: Facilitating Healing in Crime Victims*, 6 *Phoenix L. Rev.* 1017, 1025 (2013).

117 On the exclusion of whistleblowers *see*, Kate Kenny, *Whistleblowing: Toward a New Theory*, 150–159 (Harvard University Press, 2019).

118 Joyce Rothschild & Terance D. Miethe, *Whistleblower Disclosures and Management Retaliation*, 26(1) *Work Occup.* 107, 119 (1999); C. Fred Alford, *Whistleblower Narratives: The Experience of Choiceless Choice*, *Soc. Res.* 223, 228 (2007).

119 Penal Law, 5737–1977, Art. 77.

retribution against the wrongdoer, it still does very little to protect and compensate the whistleblower. This is not surprising, since the focus of criminal proceedings is whether a crime occurred, and if so, what punishment is suitable.[120] The government website providing information about employee complaints to the REA regarding employer breaches of labour law clearly states its procedural intention:

> The procedure is meant to make employers comply with labour laws and to prevent other or recurring offenses. The procedure is not meant for the following purposes: restore the status quo ante; compensate the complaining employees; give the complaining employees monetary or declaratory remedy.[121]

5.3 *Labour Law and Labour-Civil Procedure Option*

The labour-civil procedure might resolve some of the difficulties raised by the criminal procedure. In the labour-civil procedure the whistleblower is a party to the procedure.[122] She can choose whether or not to sue, and how to manage the case. This might prevent revictimization from the exclusion and lost control associated with the whistleblowing act, and may even positively affect the whistleblower's well-being, similar to the effects the civil procedure sometimes has on crime victims.[123] Moreover, the remedies offered in the labour-civil procedure are more directed to the whistleblower and contain the possibility for larger compensation and a variety of warrants, including reinstatement. Furthermore, under civil procedure in the labour court, the whistleblower can simultaneously sue for other employment infringements that sometimes accompany the retaliation but are not criminally wrong. This is useful since these infringements are often easier to prove than retaliation.

---

120 Ashworth & Zedner, *supra* note 100, at 22; James Edwards, *Theories of Criminal Law, The Stanford Encyclopedia of Philosophy* (Edward N. Zalta ed., Winter 2019 Edition) <https://plato.stanford.edu/archives/win2019/entries/criminal-law/>.

121 *See*, the Government Services and Information Website <https://www.gov.il/he/service/work-rights-violation-complaints>.

122 On the distinction between victims who participants in the proceedings and those who are full parties *see*, Douglas E. Beloof, *The Third Wave of Crime Victims: Rights, Standing, Remedy, and Review*, 2005(2) *Byu. L. Rev.* 255, 532 (2005).

123 For a similar argument regarding civil proceedings of victims of sexual crimes, *see* e.g., Nora West, *Rape in the Criminal Law and the Victim's Tort Alternative: A Feminist Analysis*, 50 *U. Toronto Fac. L. Rev.* 96, 111–1115 (1992); Yifat Bitton, *Reclaiming Power?: Women Victims Of Sexual Violence And The Civil Legal System, in Trends and Issues in Victimology* 130, 145 (Natti Ronel, K. Jaishankar and Moshe Bensimon eds., 2008). Bitton sees the promise embodied in the tort procedure for victims of sexual offenses, despite its many difficulties.

Thus, even when a whistleblower might be denied remedy on PEL grounds, she might receive it on other grounds. For example, if the retaliation ground was denied due to limitation or difficulty proving a causal-link, there might still be a remedy based on the grounds of bad faith and employer's abuse of authority.[124] A remedy may also be given for wrongful dismissal and for flaws in the hearing prior this dismissal.[125]

Additionally, under a civil-labour procedure, switching the burden of proof for the causal-link means assisting the usually weaker party in this procedure – the employee-whistleblower.[126] Under criminal procedure such assistance might undermine the presumption of innocence,[127] since it essentially shifts the prosecution's burden to prove guilt on to the usually weaker side of a criminal procedure by demanding the employer-defendant to prove they are innocent and did not violate the law.

5.4 *Structural Advantages of Israeli Labour Courts*

When dealing with civil-labour cases, the Israeli labour courts enjoy some structural advantages that might make it more procedurally suitable for whistleblowers. First, when dealing with civil cases, two public representatives with jurisdiction power preside on the bench next to the judge, and represent employees' and employers' unions.[128] When dealing with judicial matters, a public representative must,

> (…) act in accordance with his conscience and shall not regard himself owing allegiance to the organization in consultation with he was appointed or to the section of the public he represents.[129]

Public representatives can be an asset to the protection of whistleblowers. To be appointed, public representatives need to have at least five years of experience in a job or activity in the fields of labour law, employment relations, welfare, social security, economics, or public administration.[130] Thus, public

---

124 *See e.g.*, National Labour Court 25805–12–11 State of Israel v. Chumash, (Published in Nevo, Nov. 29, 2016); Tel-Aviv District Labour Court 20412–10–14 Trison v. Tel-Aviv Municipality (Published in Nevo, Dec. 27, 2017); Abergel, *supra* note 31, at para 85.

125 Gilboa Levy and Rosman, *supra* note 38, at 7.

126 *See above* at Protection of Employees Law.

127 On the presumption of innocent and its importance *see*, Andrew Ashworth, *Four threats to the presumption of innocence*, 10(4) *The International Journal of Evidence & Proof* 241, 243–248 (2006).

128 Labour Courts Law, Art. 10.

129 Labour Courts Law, Art. 16. [official translation].

130 Labour Courts Law, Art. 10.

representatives may hold relevant knowledge that is not obtained by the professional judge and that might assist in detecting employers who abuse their power and discretion.[131] Furthermore, coming from "the field," they are in a position to ensure that the interpretation of the law is compatible with social and economic developments, and not detached from actual labour relations.[132] The involvement of public representatives may enable the court to consider not only legal issues but also social and economic ones,[133] which are also pertain to the fight against corruption.[134] However, despite their potential to be a valuable tool for fighting corruption and assisting whistleblowers, public representatives rarely take an active position and usually conform with the judge.[135]

Second, in civil-labour cases, courts can be flexible and leave judges more room for discretion. First, to simplify the legal proceedings and help the judges reach a correct and just result, the courts are not officially bound to rules of evidence,[136] but rather only their principles.[137] This means that while the courts will not allow invalid or illegal evidence, they can deviate from customary legal rules and allow, for instance, hearsay evidence,[138] or the admitting of a recording transcript without the tape as evidence in certain circumstances.[139] Second, when a procedural matter is not regulated by law, judges have vast discretion and may "(...) adopt whatever course it deems best for the just handling of the case".[140] This allows the judges discretion when administrating the proceedings, for example, to allow the admission of evidence at later stages,[141]

131 Lilac Litor, Hadera Bar-Moore & Gila Menachem, *The Court and the Labour Court as Regulatory Players in the Age of Privatization*, in *Law, Society and Culture: The Role of Regulation in Israel* 349, 375 (2016). (Hebrew).

132 Guy Davidov & Reut Shemer-Begas, *Public Representatives in the Labour Court Their Function and Contribution*, in *Essays In Honour of Elika Barak-Ussoskin* 185, 194 (Stefan Adler, Yitzhak Eliasoff, Nili Arad, Guy Davidov, Sigal Davidov-Motola, Isaac Zamir, Arena Lin and Guy Mundalk ed., 2012). (Hebrew).

133 Litor, Bar-Moore & Menachem, *supra* note 131, at 375.

134 Corruption is a phenomenon that stem in social relations, culture, and economy. *See e.g.*, Kalchheim, *supra* note 62, at 54–55; Indira Carr & David Lewis, *Combating corruption through employment law and whistleblower*, 39(1) *Indus L.J.* 52, 55 (2010).

135 *See*, Davidov & Shemer-Begas, *supra* note 132, at 205–206; Ran Hermesh, *Public Representatives in the Labour Court – Partnering with Judges or Helping Professionals?*, 9 *Netanya Law Review* 229, 262–263 (2014). (Hebrew).

136 Labour Courts Law, Art. 32.

137 National Labour Court 36076-06-10 Y. Kal-Li Industries Ltd. v. Mali, in para 9–10 (published in Nevo, Dec. 9, 2010).

138 National Labour Court 1127/00 Orcz v. Danya Cebus Ltd., P.D. 37 LZ (2002) 308.

139 Y. Kal-Li, *supra* note 137.

140 Labour Courts Law, Art. 33. [official translation].

141 National Labour Court 35955-06-11 Zion Chai Buddy Appraisal v. Sharaf (published in Nevo, Jul. 20, 2011).

or allowing the practice of "Third Party Notice" that was not regulated in the Labour Courts Law.[142] This discretion and flexibility might be helpful when dealing with the often complex and hard to prove cases of whistleblowing. It is worth noting that the Ombudsman is also "not bound by rules of procedure or rules of evidence".[143]

Nevertheless, the civil procedure also has its share of hurdles and hardships for whistleblowers. It is costly, lengthy, and litigant control is still somewhat limited by the need to adhere to common legal narratives prescribed by the courts,[144] which despite their flexibility, usually follow the customary evidentiary and procedural rules.[145] In some cases the process might cause stress and anxiety, especially for vulnerable or traumatised litigants.[146] Moreover, as covered in sub-section 1(a), in Israel, whistleblowers using this option often do not have great success.

6 Conclusion: More Is Better Than One

Criminal and labour laws have different goals, different applications, and answer different needs. The focus of the criminal option in labour laws is to enhance employers' compliance, prevent offenses and, in the case of PEL, punish those responsible for the retaliation. The labour-civil procedure focuses more on the whistleblower, who is a party in the procedure, and the labour relationships, while levelling the power imbalance between the employee-whistleblower and the employer (often state, municipalities, and big companies). The labour-civil procedure enjoys flexibility and discretion that is not

142 National Labour Court 0-301 National Insurance Institute v. Radida, (1996).

143 State Comptroller Law, Art. 41(a). [official translation].

144 About the hardship's crime victims experience in civil proceedings *see e.g.*, Tamara Relis, *Civil Litigation from Litigants' Perspectives: What We Know and What We Don't Know About the Litigation Experience of Individual Litigants*, 25 *Studies in Law, Politics and Society* 151 (2002); On the hardship's caused by tort litigation for litigant who were involved in car accidents *see*, Edward J. Hickling, Edward B. Blanchard & Matthew T. Hickling, *The Psychological Impact of Litigation: Compensation Neurosis, Malingering, PTSD, Secondary Traumatization, and Other Lessons from MVAS*, 55 *DePaul L. Rev.* 617 (2006).

145 National Labour Court 148/08 Friedman Engineering and Construction Company Ltd v. Parhat, in para. 9 (published in Nevo, Dec. 08, 2008).

146 Michaela Keet, Heather Heavin & Shawna Sparrow, *Anticipating and Managing the Psychological Cost of Civil Litigation*, 34 *Windsor Yearbook of Access to Justice* 73, 78–80 (2017); Judith Lewis Herman, *The mental health of crime victims: Impact of legal intervention*, 16(2) *J. Trauma. Stress* 159, 159 (2003).

possible in the firmer and more rigid criminal procedures. The labour-civil procedure is somewhat parallel to the Ombudsman procedure, which also focuses on the whistleblower and the workplace, and aimed at offering protection for whistleblowers.

Combining multiple paths of action compensate some of the downsides each path holds on its own, enabling a more comprehensive treatment of retaliation. By providing multiple options, the whistleblower has the power to choose according to her preference, thus endowing her control pursuant to her needs and aims. Multiple options also enable us to save criminal enforcement for the more severe cases where stronger force and condemnation are needed.

The multiple options do not have to be exclusive. Already in Israeli law today we can observe some bridges between them. For example, when a whistleblower is given compensation in the civil procedure, the court can consider a fine given to the employer for retaliation, or special compensation given by the Ombudsman.[147] Similarly, when ordering a fine, the judge may consider exemplary compensation ordered in a civil-labour case, or compensation by the Ombudsman.[148] Another connection is the possibility of a civil action within the criminal law against the retaliator after he was convicted.[149]

However, the advantage of multiple options is diminished when some options are scarcely used, and others pose many hurdles. The EPMSL and the criminal procedure are hardly practiced. The civil-labour options of the PEL's and the SCL's procedures are hard to succeed. It seems this is the main symptom of the Israeli treatment regarding retaliation against whistleblowers – the separation between what theoretically is offered through the existing law, and the actual implementation of it. These paths, separately or combined, will only be successful if put to actual and attentive use. Further research is needed to understand the roots of this gap and the way to closing it.

147 Protection of Employees law, Art. 3(a1)(1).

148 Protection of Employees law, Art. 5a(b).

149 Civil law procedure regulations 5744–1984, Art. 17.

Whistleblowing and Cooperating Witnesses in Context: The Argentinian Perspective

Hugo Wortman Jofre and Ana Clara Rivero

1 Introduction

Many countries of South America present a widespread lack of compliance with the law.[1] More often than not, such disregard for the law stays unpunished, thus fostering and perpetuating disobedience.

This phenomenon can be attributed to three causes. First, the judicial powers lack the intended efficiency and effectiveness. Secondly, the penalties do not have the desired deterrent effect.[2] And thirdly, there is an increasing quantity of legal provisions that grow in complexity and severely affect the principle of legal certainty (Legislative inflation, or *inflation normative*).[3]

As to the first cause, the judicial powers in these countries work under the assumption that citizens, companies and the State abide by the law. The system also assumes that when a criminal case appears, an independent judicial system will prosecute and punish the criminal. In South America these assumptions are simple and clear, but wrong.

In Argentina, the rate of people that abide by the rule of law is extremely low.[4] This is a good example of the problems that citizens must confront when dealing with corruption in the region.

It is a common belief that human behavior is presented in a binary fashion: on one side, people who respect the law, and on the other side, people who do not. This hypothesis is exceptionally good to send to jail a small number of criminals. In other words, it is an ideal scenario in which it is preferable to

1 Carlos S. Nino, *Un país al margen de la Ley* (3rd reprint, 4th edition, Ariel, 2019) p. 20.

2 According to the Global Barometer of Corruption, in 2013, in Argentina, the 41% of the citizens would not report an act of corruption for fear of the consequences, and the other 40 % believes it would not be useful.

3 "Mesurer l'inflation normative". Conseil D'Etat. Étude présentée en assemblée générale le 3 mai 2018; Mihai Badescu, 'Legislative Inflation: An Important Cause of the Dysfunctions Existing in Contemporary Public Administration' (2018) 8 Juridical Trib 357; Dace Šulmane, '"Legislative Inflation" – An Analysis of the Phenomenon in Contemporary Legal Discourse' (2011) 4 Baltic Journal of Law & Politics 78.

4 Poder Ciudadano de abril de 1992, encuesta de Gallup Argentina (www.poderciudadano.org).

 | DOI:10.1163/9789004459816_006

believe that in our society the ninety percent of the people respect the law and only a ten percent of them do not.

In this ideal, hypothetical context, all social participants (government officials, citizens, suppliers, taxpayers, bankers, etc.) obey the rule of law and the justice works properly. Consequently, the judicial system is very efficient in its fight against corruption and in its efforts to prevent it. If those who do not respect the law are sent to jail, then all corruption problems are solved.

Even so, the real context in South America is quite different. Beyond this binary profile of people, there is a third, important category: those individuals who are 'honest but sinful'.[5] This situation provokes a new ethical category in organizations and communities in which all these types of people co-exist. In fact, the 'honest but sinful' people are our potential whistleblowers or cooperating witnesses.

On top of that, the only way to fight against corruption efficiently in our region is to consider that people respect the law depending on the context. On this regard, there is global consensus on the essential nature of providing safety to those who have information or relevant data for the prosecution of certain crimes. Witnesses, whether whistleblowers or cooperating witnesses, need to feel safe to give testimony without fear of any kind of reprisals or being afraid of situations that may put their integrity at risk.

In South America, persons who comes forward and speaks up, are normally ill advised or in great danger. For that reason, it is necessary to create programs to provide them with special protection, so that they feel safe and able to provide a full and comprehensive testimony.

Moreover, the importance of an adequate system of protection to victims, witnesses, plaintiffs and defendants is most evident in those cases which, due to their complexity, require the contribution of information and evidence obtained by the statement of witnesses or people who have taken actual knowledge of crimes.

These types of protective programs are essential, especially because witnesses, whistleblowers and cooperating witnesses are usually the ones that really know the details of the criminal action under investigation, and therefore, they could contribute to the process with valuable evidence that might otherwise never become known.

---

5 Poder Ciudadano (an Argentinian NGO, local chapter of Transparency International) made another survey together with 'Gallup' Argentina (in which around 1000 people from Capital City and the province of Buenos Aires have participated) that reproduces the same results.

Besides, the right of anyone to report any act that may eventually involve an inappropriate behavior is part of the fundamental right to freedom of expression; what is more, it is the commitment of every citizen with democracy, reflected in the will of every individual to protect and fight for justice, truth, equality and transparency.

As to the second aspect related to the failure of criminal law, for the penalties do not have the desired deterrent effect, it is first worth mentioning that punishment does not arrive early, and it is especially strict with low-income people. Scholars researching the length of the judicial processes investigating corruption in Argentina estimated that 15 years were the reasonable time to finish these types of cases.[6] Additionally, many recent corruption cases involved judges and prosecutors that allegedly protected drug dealers and illegal gambling criminals.[7] Owing to this, people trust in justice less and less.

As to the last point, it should be noted that there is an enormous quantity of legal regulations in these matters. For instance, there is a Code of Criminal Procedures, heavily focused on the central role of prosecutors,[8] which is only applied in two provinces as a mode of pilot project; the rest of the country applies a different National Code of Criminal Procedures, based on the central, role of judges. With regards to the rights of cooperating witnesses, for example, there are 17 different legal systems applied among 24 provinces, many of them with double or contradictory regulations.[9]

On the whole, the context in which the cooperation institute is applied in Argentina is quite complex and it is difficult to incorporate *common law* regulations in a country which has adopted the civil law legal system. Moreover, after these regulations are finally introduced, problems of interpretation start to emerge and affect their effectiveness.

In the meantime, the discussion in Argentina is centered around the legality of testimonies, while in other countries, such as in the United States, the Department of Justice supports cooperating witnesses – according to the *qui tam* action – to recover illegal funds. Moral debates versus pragmatism, this is the gap that divides our realities.[10]

---

6 http://acij.org.ar/sin_corrupcion/wp-content/uploads/2016/11/Poder-Los-proceso-judiciales-en-materia-de-corrupcion.pdf.

7 News stories about the Judge of Oran and Prosecutors of Rosario and San Isidro. Scapolan case: https://www.pagina12.com.ar/282336-la-causa-contra-claudio-scapolan-fiscal-de-san-isidro. And Serjal case: https://www.telam.com.ar/notas/202008/497742-renuncia-patricio-serjal-fiscal-rosario-lazos-los-monos.html.

8 Law No. 27063.

9 USAL, investigation: "Cooperation in argentine criminal process. National and provincial systems. Background, evolution and future", 7.30.2018.

10 The *False Claims Act* (31 U.S.C. Sections 3729 through 3733).

I will start this work by unraveling the concept of the legal figures of witnesses, whistleblowers and cooperating witnesses, and I will analyse the most important aspects of the last two.

Then, I will expose the main legal complications derived from the incorporation of these common law institutes to our civil law system and will analyse the essential discussions around them.

2 The Role of Whistleblowers and Cooperating Witnesses

2.1 *Witnesses, Whistleblowers and Cooperating Witnesses*

One of the main pieces of evidence in criminal investigations is witness testimony.

This means the contribution to justice of everything a person saw, heard, or simply perceived from a criminal act, whether the person was involved in the crime or not.

A person that provides relevant testimony about the commission of a certain criminal offense can be involved in the process in highly different manners. The first possibility is to be a mere witness, in which the only involvement in the criminal process is to provide the authorities with her version of the facts, from her perspective. The individual can also be a whistleblower, as a special category of witnesses. That is to say,

> An employee who alleges wrongdoing by his or her employer of the sort that violates public law or tends to injure a considerable number of people. The employer can be public or private. Whistleblowers often relay information to law enforcement and other government agencies.[11]

Finally, the person who is involved in the crime and decides to provide relevant information about it is defined as a cooperating witness.[12]

The duty to report a crime is not mandatory in every country. For instance, in Argentina, procedural law only requires public officials and health professionals to report crimes they have witnessed. Besides, whether the person is or not involved in the perpetration of the crime becomes irrelevant, since there

11 'Whistleblower' (*LII / Legal Information Institute*) <https://www.law.cornell.edu/wex/whistleblower> accessed 11 April 2021. In same way: https://www.oecd.org/corruption/Committing-to-Effective-Whistleblower-Protection-Highlights.pdf.

12 Maier, Julio B. 2004. Derecho Procesal Penal. Fundamentos T 1. 2da Edicion. Editorial del Puerto. Pag 188. Critical point of view of intitute.

is no special treatment for those who cooperate with the authorities, and thus they take a high personal risk by doing so.

In an attempt to solve this problem, in 2003 the country enacted Law No. 25764, which created the National Program for the Protection of Witnesses and Cooperating Witnesses. This program stipulates security measures for both, witnesses and cooperating witnesses who "(...) had cooperated transcendentally and efficiently in a judicial investigation (...) related to (...) kidnapping, extortion, drug trafficking and terrorism".[13] These measures seek to prevent witnesses and cooperating witnesses from suffering any harm derived from their collaboration in criminal investigations, although excluding numerous offences such as frauds against the State and all types of corruption.

Moreover, the law only refers to federal crimes leaving each 24 provinces to regulates their protection system autonomously and uncoordinated from the national government.[14] The rest of offences are submitted to the general rules of the Procedural Code,[15] which does not contemplate any special protection for either whistleblowers or witnesses. Even more, it establishes the possibility for witnesses to be detained and carried to court by law enforcement agents in case they refuse to go voluntarily. There is also a lack of protection for witnesses in terms of retaliation such as work dismissal, threats or any other civil or criminal harm derived from their collaboration with the judicial system.

The lack of special mechanisms to protect whistleblowers, witnesses and cooperating witnesses is, at least, problematic. In 2006 Jorge Julio Lopez,[16] who was a transcendental witness to a criminal investigation related to the commission of crimes against humanity in Argentina, disappeared. From that moment onwards, authorities started to warn about the grave risk ran by witnesses of human rights trials. For that reason, Argentina created the Program for Truth and Justice,[17] which aimed, among other things, at coordinating with diverse bodies of the State to strengthen the process of truth and justice regarding the crimes against humanity committed during the last coup d'état. The coordination efforts also comprehended provisions to guarantee the protection and security of witnesses, victims, lawyers, judicial employees (and their family members) that play a part in such criminal investigations.

13 Law No. 25764, art. 1.

14 In Argentina, there are 17 province systems of protection mechanisms.

15 Art. 240, "*... toda persona tiene la obligación de concurrir al llamamiento judicial ...*".

16 Graziano, Miguel (2013). En el cielo nos vemos. La historia de Jorge Julio López. Ed. Continente.

17 Executive Power of the Nation, Decree No. 606/2007.

At the international level, there is consensus that witnesses, whistleblowers and cooperating witnesses should receive a special treatment by the authorities,[18] to avoid threats or any other negative consequences derived from their contribution to justice. The main purpose is clear, to stimulate this type of cooperation and to contribute to eradicate normative deviation. Unfortunately, Argentinian lacks a mechanism of integral protection for witnesses, cooperating witnesses and whistleblowers.

2.2 *The Challenges of Regulating Cooperating Witnesses and Whistleblowers*

'Cooperating witnesses' has been widely popular in the *common law* tradition and has recently been introduced in the civil law. Prior to its introduction, Argentina incorporated two other legal figures from the *common law* system. Mainly the pretrial *probation* procedure,[19] and the deferred adjudication procedure.[20] Both legal figures require a negotiation between the accused, the defense lawyer and the prosecutor. The interpretation of these figures in the local legal system has also been a matter of controversy both in case-law and doctrine.[21] The main aspects of the debates have always been centered around the role of the State, the accused and the victims in relation to the agreement to reduce punishment in exchange for information.

Although it will be developed further in this work, it is worth mentioning that some scholars and courts have considered the State could not and should

18 UNCAC, articles 8, 13 and 33; OECD, Anti-Bribery Convention, 2009 Recommendation for Further Combating Bribery of Foreign Public Officials in International Business Transactions, Section IX.iii. and Section X.C.v., and Annex II to the Recommendation, Good Practice Guidance on Internal Controls, Ethics and Compliance, Section A.11.ii; OECD Recommendation on Improving Ethical Conduct in the Public Service, Principle 4; Council of Europe Civil Law Convention on Corruption, Article 9; Council of Europe Criminal Law Convention on Corruption, Article 22 and Inter-American Convention against Corruption, Article III (8).

19 National Criminal Code, art. 76 *bis*.

20 Procedural Criminal Code, art. 431 *bis*.

21 See cases "Osorio Sosa, Apolonio", 23/12/1997, particularly the position of Judge Mario Magariños, from the Oral Criminal Tribunal No. 23 of the Autonomous City of Buenos Aires N°, case "Arrojo, Gustavo Eduardo s/ robo", 19/05/2016, (file No. 69.295/2013). Likewise, see case Urrutia Valencia, Marcelo Alejandro", 20/03/2011, particularly the position of Judge Luis Niño, from the Oral Criminal Tribunal No.20 of the Autonomous City of Buenos Aires.

not accept accused individuals to give up their defense right on the basis of an agreement with the prosecution.[22]

This line of interpretation considers that the State has a paternalistic role which overrules the will of the defendant. In other words, human beings are not free to self-determination and the election of their destiny. Nor are they free to exercise their right to freely express themselves before a judge. The critique position against this moral superiority of the State is centered on the amplitude of such freedom. After all, the State, and particularly the judicial system, is the only one who can determine under which conditions the defendant will cooperate.

On the other hand, while the EU and the international community have recognized the distinction between whistleblowers and general witnesses,[23] whistleblowers have not been recognized within the Argentinian legal system as a distinctive set of witnesses.

This lack of recognition and awareness has triggered a severe loophole with little to no protection to whistleblowers. If there is consensus on the distinction between whistleblowers as deserving special treatment, the general provisions on witnesses would fall short to provide the due safeguard.

2.3 *Leading Case Involving Argentina*[24]

In 2012, the Vice-president of Argentina, Amado Boudou, was accused in a case of corruption. He presumably participated through a figurehead in the acquisition of the company 'Ciccone Calcográfica S.A.', an enterprise dedicated to the printing of Argentinian bills. The trial was led by federal criminal justice Ariel Lijo.

In 2014, Guido Forcieri, by that time the Director of the World Bank for Argentina and the former Cabinet Chief of Mr. Boudou, was also accused for the same misconduct.

During this investigation, two officers of the World Bank, identified as DR and DS accessed to the computer records of the institution and proved that Mr. Forcieri took a trip to Argentina to comply with a judicial summon after

22 "Zur Kritik des amerikanischen Strafprozessmodells". En: FS für Gerhard Fezer zum 70. Geburstag am 29. Oktober 2008. Berlin: De Gruyter Recht, 2008, p. 564 y ss, defines these agreements as "the downfall of the german legal culture" and considers that in this case, the accused is on a vulnerable position which leads to an inquisitory system.

23 Ragues I Valles, Ramón. "Whistleblowing. Una aproximación desde el derecho penal". Marcial Pons. 213.

24 https://tribunal.worldbank.org/sites/tribunal.worldbank.org/files/Judgments%20and%20Orders/DR%20and%20DS%20v.%20IFC%20550.pdf.

several refusals. Still, in the middle of the trip he decided to suspend his appearance before the justice and returned to Washington.

The two World Bank officers gave the information to a research journalist of one of the most important newspapers of the country. The journalist published a news denouncing this failure to comply with the judicial summon before Justice Ariel Lijo.

These facts derived in an investigation led by the authorities of the Bank that concluded in a sanction imposed by the area of human resources, consisting in a suspension and loss of salary. DR and DS appealed this sanction to the Administrative Court of the Bank. They alleged that the decision was imposed by not taking into account they were whistleblowers (regulated in the Staff Rule 8.02, of the Protection and Procedures for Reporting Misconduct (Whistleblowing), paragraph 4, External Reporting). They claimed that the information was provided to collaborate with Argentina in an investigation on the possible corruption of its own public functionaries as to avoid legal obstacles.

The Court of the World Bank dictated its judgement on 4th November 2016. The Court considered that the conduct of DR and DS violated the rules of confidentiality for staff members by revealing information about the travel itinerary of Mr. Forcieri (Principle 3.1.d).

Before this judgement was issued, the Bank stablished transparency policies with diverse channels of internal and external reports. The latter ones were not prohibited for employees, especially when they witnessed or intend to avoid threats to health of public security in a Bank operation and to prevent national or international law infringements.

Regarding this, the Court considered that not using these type of reporting procedures was justified in a case of risk of a loss of evidence or coercion to the reporting person or if the internal channel was ineffective. The Court concluded that these requirements were not present in the policies stablished by the Bank (see paragraph 102 of the judgement).

It goes without saying that the most important argument of the Court was that the leadership role of the Bank in the fight against corruption among the world and the regulations of the Code of Conduct (paragraph 3) could easily led DR and DS to consider that the non-compliance of Mr. Forcieri implied risk to the bank operations. This is due to the fact that the rules of conduct stipulate that the Directors of this institution should observe the law of every jurisdiction in which they work as to prevent privileges, abuses or immunities derived from the position (see paragraph 90 of the judgement).

With these arguments, the Court reversed the sanction imposed to DR and DR and ordered to remove from their personal files any reference to this investigation.

3 Essential Discussions about Cooperating Witnesses

The figure of cooperating witnesses does not exist in Argentina as it does in Europe or the United States. Moreover, as it has been developed in the previous section, the legal protection of witnesses and whistleblowers is highly limited.

The local legal system is more focused on the individual guilt of the cooperator as the central objective in the fight against crime, even more so since there is a strong public claim to clarify high-profile acts of corruption that have happened in Argentina.

Discussions around cooperating witnesses in this jurisdiction are like in many other parts of the world.[25] The main controversy surrounding cooperating witnesses is the possibility of a defendant to renounce to her constitutional rights in exchange of a benefit regarding an alternative end, other than punishment, to the criminal process.[26]

This has not been exempted from criticism, such as the disregard of the right to legal counseling, the protection against self-incrimination, equality of arms and due process.

3.1 *The Right to a Fair Trial*

The right to a fair trial is the most essential principle.[27] Among other rights, it comprehends the right to be heard in trial, to understand their charges, to have time to present and produce evidence in her favor, and to examine witnesses against her.[28] The whole system of the criminal trial relies on the idea that the individual must resist the *ius puniendi*.[29]

For that reason, any form of cooperation between the defendant and the prosecution ought to be carried out with the intervention of the defense lawyer to properly evaluate the risks, advantages and disadvantages of every decision.[30]

25 See Constitutional Court of Belgium: decision No. 2013-679 DC, 4/12/ 2013 – Observations of the Government, related to a consult submitted by 60 senators against a law against tax fraud y economic and financial crime. See also Constitutional Tribunal of Spain, case No. 69/01, “Marey”.

26 In the case n° 9608/2018/100 (Sala de la Camara Nacional de Casación Penal, Registro 1663/20) against the current vice president of Argentina, Cristina F de Kirchner, different defense lawyers questioned the lawfulness of the testimonies of some cooperators by arguing a disregard of her right to a fair trial. Also see Law No. 27304, art. 6.

27 Maier, Julio B.J., *Derecho Procesal Penal, I Fundamentos*, Ed. Del Puerto, 2004, p. 547.

28 See Carrió, Alejandro D., *Garantías Constitucionales en el proceso penal*, Ed. Hammurabi, Buenos Aires, 1994, p. 65.

29 The art. 14, 3. d) of the International Covenant on Civil and Political Rights.

30 Law No. 27.304, in its art. 10, stipulates that the judge will hear the parties of the process and guarantee that the cooperator has a proper knowledge about the implications of the agreement.

As a result, the forms and procedures preceding the celebration of an agreement of cooperation acquires a transcendental relevance. These forms and procedures should assume a logical sequence of comprehension, collaboration and celebration (C + C + C).

Comprehension implies both cognitive and volitional aspects of the human and legal dimension about what it means to start collaborating with the judicial system. This phase involves a process in which the person has to understand that cooperation implies a commitment to contribute to the process with useful evidence and also making the necessary efforts to convince that the information provided is relevant and true. Moreover, comprehension means to understand the personal and familial risks which could derive from this type of agreement. Psychological and economic assistance should be considered by judges. During the whole phase of comprehension, medical cabinets could be useful to clarify doubts about the level of understanding acquired by the person involved in the agreement.

Collaboration belongs to the next phase, involving a conscious and voluntary decision to cooperate, which definitely constitutes the major change. From this moment, a cooperating witness should realize that it will be necessary to make every reasonable human effort to present useful evidence to the investigation. In a process which is defined by the trinomial of a thesis (prosecutor), antithesis (defense) and synthesis (judgment), the agreement should transform the second phase into a new 'thesis of the cooperator'. Instead of trying to refute the thesis of the prosecution, the thesis of the cooperator would support it by providing new evidence. Still, should this 'thesis of the cooperator' be considered an act of defense or an act of accusation?

The 'thesis of the cooperator' is a defense strategy built on the basis of a normative rule, which implies supporting everything or part of the accusing thesis. However, this does not mean that the cooperator is transformed into a claimant against the rest of defendants. Actually, within this mechanism, only one of the defendants could defend himself by stating that the legal and factual claims of the prosecution are totally or partially true. What is more, the defendant is able to dissent with part of the claims of the prosecution, such as, her intervention in the facts, or decide to just partially cooperate with it.

It is an autonomous decision within the spectrum of tools that a defendant has to exercise her right to a fair trial. The certainty about the guilts or innocence of a defendant is only determined with a verdict. During the criminal procedure everyone should be free to decide what is its best defense strategy.

The third phase, the celebration, consists in the positive or negative evaluation that the prosecutor makes on the evidence presented by the cooperator, the homologation of the judge and the subsequent acquisition (or not) of the benefit of the reduction of punishment. It constitutes the final stage of the process of cooperation. This procedural moment could be laid out in different ways, e.g., giving more discretional faculties to the prosecutor and less to the judges or *vice versa*. Still, the only purpose of the phase is the utilitarian assessment of the cooperation by the bodies in charge of the criminal investigation.

3.2 *Self-Incrimination*

The right to a legal defense involves the prohibition of compelling an accused person to declare against himself (prohibition of self-incrimination, article 18 of the National Constitution of the Republic of Argentina). The principal aim is to prevent the accused from a coerced declaration that could be used as evidence against him. As it is written in the National Constitution, it is forbidden to oblige a person to "declare against himself".[31] Furthermore, this guarantee does not only involve "not compelling" but also obliges the judge to provide the accused with the knowledge of his right to remain in silence without any negative consequence.[32]

It does not mean that the accused is not allowed to a conscious and willing self-incrimination. That is to say, this guarantee should be understood as a right to be protected from a coerced declaration against ourselves, but not as an obligation that prevent us from freely declaring against ourselves.

Related to this is the compulsory situation of an accused person, when a confession is obtained by police pressure, which was deeply studied in case law and doctrine since the known case "Miranda Rules", from the Supreme Court of the United States of America.[33] This precedent was issued in an institutional context which was crossed by two opposite positions, a conservatory one, that intended to consent police abuses, and a more liberal posture that seeks to protect individual rights. In its final version, the Miranda Rules stipulate that the responsibility to guarantee an effective right to legal defense is of the prosecutor.

In order to validate a confession, it is necessary to conduct a strict test which involves more than the simple verification of a mere absence of coercion. It is also essential for this requisite to be determined by the prosecutor or in some cases by the judge, who must guard for the total validity of the procedural and penal guarantees that protect an accused person.

---

31 The origin of this norm is in the v Amendment of the Carta Magna of the United States, which stipulates "… no person shall be compelled in any criminal case to be a witness against himself …".

32 Carrió (n 28) p. 478/9.

33 Case "Miranda vs. Arizona", Supreme Court of US, 384 US 436 (1966).

In involves an evaluation of the "communication" maintained by the accused person (an analysis which is highly different from a digital fingerprint of a blood withdrawal); therefore, the determination of its validity requires the "issuer" of the message to provide the receiver with a willing communication, with all the necessary legal assistance that would allow him to understand the implications of his acts.

This type of willingness is the one that should be accomplished in the arrangement of any cooperation agreement. Still, this position is far from being unanimous.

For instance, authors like Sancinetti claimed – in the parliamentary discussion about the Law No. 27.304 – that in these types of agreements the accused person will always be subject to coercion. He sustained that the mere fact of being submitted to a criminal process, not being yet guilty, could lead an accused person to believe that, if the terms of the agreement are not accepted, his procedural situation could be aggravated.

This theory – also sustained by other scholars[34] – affirms that the enormous difference of power between the State and the accused person prevents from the possibility of any willingness of a procedural agreement.

Another discussion that comes from this posture is related to the following dilemma: should the State promote the reduction of punishment or should it remain expectant to the arrival of a potential cooperator.

When it comes to this matter, there should be more flexible rules, and the prosecutors and judges should establish the whole necessary measures to fathom the willingness of the cooperator.[35] The mere fact that the negotiation of an agreement is made by the State does not make the act invalid *per se*, as it is necessary to perform an integral evaluation of the decision.

3.3 *Equality Right*

The Argentinian constitution stipulates that "All inhabitants are equal under the law …".[36] This assertion opens multiple debates regarding its reach. Broadly speaking, it implies that every person should be as much autonomous as

34 See Rusconi, Maximiliano, *Witness Crown and Criminal Law. New ways to fight organized criminality or the inquisition of the new millennium?* Available at https://www.hammurabi.com.ar/rusconi-maximiliano-arrepentidos/, last accessed 25 May 2021.

35 In similar terms, Mirenxtu Corcoy Bidasolo at the conference "The Cooperating Witness", Faculty of Law of the University of Buenos Aires, 12 April 18 (http://www.derecho.uba.ar/noticias/2018/conferencia-sobre-arrepentido-y-derecho-penal-economico-presentacion-del-libro-responsabilidad-de-la-persona-juridica-y-compliance).

36 National Constitution of the Republic of Argentina, article 16.

possible in his decision-making process; always without imposing sacrifices to others or affecting the autonomy of others.

The Interamerican Court of Human Rights has said that,

> the concept of liberty and the possibility of all human beings to self-determination and to choose freely the options and circumstances that give meaning to their life, according to their own choices and beliefs is a basic human right which belongs to the attributes of any person, and it is reflected in the whole American Convention.[37]

There are certain characteristics that norms should have, to guarantee equality.[38] Still, these characteristics do not solve the dilemma that exists with regard to the content a norm should have as to be considered egalitarian.

The exercise of these rights and its judicial acknowledgement in cases of legal controversies determine a model of justice that balance the differences and tend to avoid possible inequalities. At the same time, it implies that individuals cannot be used as instruments in benefit of others, and there are universal consensuses (known as the universal law, from Kant), that tends to solve these types of conflicts.

These norms are useful to solve the inequalities of the system. Thus, together with them, there are certain principles which are identified as other rules and also deserve abidance.[39]

With regard to these principles, the central thesis considers that they are different than norms. Principles refer to justice and equality, they bring reasons to decide in one sense or another. Between principles and norms there is a logical distinction. With regard to equality, Dworkin draws on his concept of *ethical individualism*, a concept based on the principle of individual life's success and special responsibility. The first one requires the government to adopt the necessary legal and administrative measures to prevent its citizens from a destiny that depends on what he defines as « circumstances ». While the second one aims the governments to promote that the destiny of the citizens responds to their « elections »; thus, we are especially responsible for the success of our existence. According to authors like Gargarella,[40] society should allow individuals to be responsible of the results from their preferences and ambitions.

37 CIDH, "Artavia Murillo vs. Costa Rica", 28/11/2012.

38 Nino, Carlos, *Ocho lecciones sobre ética y derecho, para pensar la democracia*, Ed. Siglo XXI, Buenos Aires, 2013, p. 71/74.

39 Dworkin, Ronald, *Los derechos en serio*, Ed. Ariel Derecho, Barcelona, 1989, p. 22; Rawls, John, *Teoría de la Justicia* (Fondo de Cultura Económica, 1993).

40 Roberto Gargarella. "Las Teorías de la Justicia después de Rawls", Paidos, 1999.

Finally, Dworkin also encourages the neutrality of an egalitarian state by not rewarding or forbidding any private activity on the base of an assumed superior ethic.

Moreover, authors like Nino affirm that considering others as equals means that the autonomy of the will of every person is unique and unrepeatable.[41] Nino understands this allows everyone to plan their life and to adopt their own ideals of excellence. By following Rawls, he affirms everyone has the right to a maximum liberty as long as it is not obtained at the expense of the liberties of others.

By taking these theories into account, is easy to explain that the incorporation of the cooperating witness in the Argentinian law involves providing the defendant with another alternative among his procedural choices. Therefore, it gives him a relative freedom to choose her luck in the criminal process.[42]

In the words of authors like Dworkin, the defendant is owner of this success or failure. A concept of equality which is understood in that sense is useful to rebuild the social structure and to achieve criminal agreements.

Moreover, the state can implement public policies of inducement of these types of actions; according to authors like Nino, "there should be incentives which modify the preference of the actors, such as immunities or other positive rewards to those who report unlawful acts".[43]

The laws that introduce these policies should be general rules, non-retroactive, clear, secure and with permanent application.

This means that any legal rule on cooperation including a strict list of offences could be criticized for affecting the constitutional extent of the equality right.[44]

As previously explained, this was subject to discussion in the law debate in the Senate. In that opportunity, Sancinetti postulated the infringement of the equality principle because those who possess valuable information were in a better position than those who do not, thus entailing benefits only for the first ones. According to this author, the law of cooperating witnesses leads to an absolute inequality, because the principal offenders have access to more

41 Nino, Carlos, *Un país al margen de la ley*, Ed. Ariel, Buenos Aires, 2011, p. 165.

42 Francisco Alonso-Fernández "*El hombre libre y sus sombras. Una antropología de la libertad*" Editorial Anthropos. (2006); Antonio Millán Puelles "Fundamentos de Filosofía", Ed. Rialp SA. 1978, *pag. 377 sobre Libertad.*

43 Nino, op. cit., p. 228 (Un país al margen de la ley, Editorial Ariel 2005).

44 Usually, crimes against humanity are excluded from the systems of cooperation. This could violate the principle of equality.

useful information and more possibilities to be benefited than those who did not occupy an important role in the criminal organization.[45]

This critique should be answered by stating that equality is not limited to guarantee identical rights to every citizen. I have already stated that the autonomous will of every individual should be maximized as long as it is not obtained at the expense of other's liberties.

Besides, the solution to this problem should not be the limitation or reduction of the individual autonomy when a person decides to cooperate. On the contrary, there should be corrective rules (acting as counterbalances) of these potential inequalities without setting aside the benefits of the institute.

This happens in the Argentinian law, which establishes a rule that prevents the ringleaders of a criminal organization from access to the benefits of cooperation.[46] Moreover, excluding those who possess more information or those who are more committed to the criminal activity and even stipulating time limits within the process to access to the benefit prevents the disturbance of defense strategies of other accused individuals (cooperators or non-cooperators).

In other words, respect for equality is not accomplished by suppressing options which restrict the autonomy of the individual but setting mechanisms that guarantee a system in which these options are not obtained at the cost of other's minor liberties. As previously stated, these counterbalances could be limits to the operating hierarchy of the cooperators, time limits within the process to access to the benefit, etc. The Law No. 27304 in its article 3, for example, stipulates the possibility to negotiate with a cooperating witness precludes when the investigation phase is closed, and the trial phase begins. The aim is to guarantee that the rest of the accused individuals have the right to know and contradict the factual platform of the accusation. The element of surprise of a cooperating witness in the trial could affect the principle of equality.

Finally, the introduction of the cooperating witness does not alter the general procedural rules of evidence assessment. Like every other piece of evidence, this testimony of the cooperating witness should be analyzed under this same system of assessment. The only difference relies on the fact that it comes from someone who has participated in the offence and knows the diverse aspects of the criminal organization.

This is other argument that helps to dismiss the idea of lack of equality, because the only modification in the process is the amount and quality of evidence which will be evaluated under the general principles on the matter.

---

45 http://www.senado.gov.ar/prensa/14228/noticias pp. 67/74.

46 Law No. 27.304, art. 3.

3.4 *Due, Regular and Legal Process*

The article 18 of the Argentinian constitution establishes a mandatory legal trial before judgement. Broadly speaking, this implies that every time a tribunal adopts a decision regarding an accusation, it should be supported by the necessary evidence. In other words, it should be adopted on the base of a certain and concrete factual premise. Hence the idea of temporal mediacy of the criminal punishment, which means that the State cannot exercise direct coercion. It should be the result of a decision that puts an end to a legal proceeding and authorizes the State to impose a sanction. Punishment cannot be randomly imposed.

Criminal proceeding means the "legal protection of the defendant" and the criminal procedural law is a regulatory law of the National Constitution. The so-called *due process of law* in the US legal system contains general rules – also stipulated in our National Constitution – which regulates the validity and interpretation of the law. Like the *fair trial* in the English *common law*, it implies the guarantee of an impartial and loyal trial, establishing equal opportunities to every person submitted to trial (specifically stipulated in the article 6 of the European Convention on Human Rights).

The cooperating witness involves diverse discussions about the principle of 'equality of arms' in the criminal process.[47] Indeed, apart from the logic of accusation-defense (thesis and antithesis), a new actor emerges and modifies the traditional dynamic of the criminal process. As it has been pointed out before, the cooperator is an accused person that has taken the decision to help in the verification of the prosecutor's thesis. On this regard, it was also stated that the strategy of cooperation of the defendant should be understood as "her" strategy of defense at trial. This strategy is not part of the legal defense strategy of the rest of the accused individuals.

Besides, it is a free and willing election of a certain path, a defense right which is contained in the current legislation, therefore, not illegal. As previously stated, it is the reflection of the right to self-determination.

Still, it should be determined if the willingness of the decision is at stake because of the offer of a punishment reduction made by the State. A dispassionate observer could reflect in the following terms: a situation in which the accused person decides to confess without receiving anything in exchange

---

47 García, Luis M., "El Principio de Igualdad de Armas y los nuevos requerimientos (El derecho al control de la prueba introducida en el juicio. La incorporación de actas y la ocultación de la identidad de testigos, informantes e investigadores bajo cubierta)". *El dial.com* DC.69: http://www.eldial.com.ar/nuevo/archivo-doctrina-detalle-tc.asp?archivo=nt000225.asp&pie=DC69%3Cbr%3E&direc=2.

is highly different than another person whose decision is motivated by the reduction of the penalty.

According to Sancinetti for example,[48] it could also be argued that this confession would serve to this 'occasional' offer only if it is considered as 'useful' by the judicial officers in charge of its evaluation. According to Sancinetti, this system facilitates the conviction of innocents and promotes the reduction of penalties to those who are guilty. Besides, it turns the criminal action into a commodity that can be subjected to trade. As stated by authors like Jakobs,[49] "If a person acts following his interests instead of categories, the parameter is determined by the market and not by justice. The most desired compensation is paid with a major quantity; without compensation, there is not even one day of punishment reduction".

These questionings lead to reflect about the theories of punishment. In this matter, authors like Sancinetti affirm that in Germany the current dominant position is the positive general prevention theory.[50] According to this theory, the penalty serves to stabilize conduct expectations. The author of the offense compromises the validity of the norm. He expresses, similarly to Hegel, that the norm is not worth for the author (if so, he would not commit the offense). Thus, he damages the validity of the norm. The contra-factual reaction of society with a penalty reinforces the idea that this norm is still valid as a parameter of the proper behavior; that society is in the right side and the offender in the wrong opposite side. This message of communication and answer is imposed at expenses of the author.

This theory is highly extended today and sustained by diverse scholars such as Jakobs, Hassemer and Frister. Still, previous to the expression "positive general prevention", Von Liszt has already argued on the same base.[51]

Following Sancinetti's theory, the compositional model does not ensure the justifications of punishment because social compensation would not be

---

48 Sancinetti. Marcelo. "Avenimiento o Mediación. ¿La pena como objeto de negocios jurídicos? Available at http://www.pensamientopenal.com.ar/doctrina/38164-avenimiento-y-mediacion-pena-objeto-negocios-juridicos.

49 Jakobs, *Rücktritt als Tatänderung versus allgemeines Nachtatverhalten*, in ZStW, t. 104 (1992), p. 82, esp. p. 86 (there is a Spanish version from Enrique Peñaranda Ramos in *Jakobs, Estudios de Derecho Penal*, Civitas, Madrid, 1997, p. 325 ss., esp. p. 328).

50 Roxin, Claus. "Desarrollos actuales de las ciencias criminales en Alemania", Cedal, Göttingen University Press 2018, *Complicidad en el asesinato por medio del servicio en el campo de concentración de Auschwitz*, p. 206, punto III.

51 Cf. v. Liszt, *La idea de fin en el Derecho penal*, transl. E. Aimone Gibson, Edeval, Valparaíso, 1984, pp. 128, 129 and 131. It is the Spanish version of the known "Program of the Universirt of Marburgo"(Presidency speech read in 1882): Marburger Universitätsprogramm, reedited the following year as *Der Zweckgedanke im Strafrecht*, en ZStW, t. 3 [1883], p. 1.

included in the aim of the proceeding. However, the reaffirmation of the validity of the norm would not disappear if taking into account the explanation of Jakobs, who affirms that the compensation of the author implies a recognition of the validity of the norm and a public quality. On the other side, Sancinetti pretends to relativize the words of Jakobs by affirming that the clarification "I do not consider this rule as a catastrophe" suggests that an intuitive vision should tend to conformism.

On the contrary, Jakobs seems to be consistent with the idea that the aim of the penalty is to "reaffirm the validity of the norm" and that "... the aim of the penalty is the maintenance of the norm as an orientation model to social contracts".[52]

Due process should guarantee the application of rational rules for a fair punishment. As it was developed in this section, the institute of cooperation does not disturb the general rules of the adversarial procedure and could even be understood as the recognition of the validity of the norm. None will cooperate to restore a legal order if not starting with the recognition of the validity of its validity.

3.5 *Essential Discussions about Whistleblowers*

Whistleblowers are still being regulated under the general rules of the criminal procedure and lack of a special protection, neither against an unfair employment dismissal nor against any other threat.

As it was previously developed in this work, there are no special legal provisions in Argentina in order to protect whistleblowers. As a consequence, the main problem in our country relies in the legal vacuum there is this matter and the urgent need for a proper legislation.

Another important issue is that Argentina is a federal country and its legal provisions should be stipulated in each province in their own Procedural Codes. It was also mentioned that this have provoked that over 24 provinces there are 17 legal systems that stablish diverse legal provisions, focusing particularly on the protection of witnesses of certain type of offenses without any consideration of their job stability.

Related to this is that the also mentioned Law No. 25764 which created a national program to protect witnesses of highly specific criminal cases (kidnapping, coercion, drugs and terrorism) excluding for instance corruption and transnational crimes. Besides, this program presents structural failures. It lacks of a mechanism to guarantee job and economic stability for witnesses. To mention an example, article 5.d of this law stipulates that "In any case the

52 Jakobs, Günter, *Derecho Penal. Parte General*, Ed. Marcial Pons, Argentina, 1995. p. 13.

economic assistance will be granted for more than six months". It is an honest contradiction as the criminal processes in Argentina tend to last years, not months, leading the witnesses to reach to decisive trial phases without any type of special protection.

Recently, with the inaction of Law No. 27401 on criminal responsibility of legal persons, enterprises have started to create their own Compliance Programs (article 23), including in it an Ethics Code. Besides, the Anticorruption Office of Argentina has propitiated the inclusion of rules orientated to avoid retaliation against reporting people.[53] This seems to be a clear step in the correct direction, still highly limited in its practical impacts.

3.6 *Current Situation in Argentina*

Whistleblowing and cooperating imply the disclosure or reporting of certain crimes, such as corruption, in which the State plays an important role in its fight. Therefore, proper legislation and measures are needed to be taken in order to promote these actions and to provide security to whistleblowers and cooperating witnesses.

The fight against corruption is legitimate and has a high level of public interest. It should not be forgotten that corruption in any field affects everyone; it is not expected that people would remain silent for fear of reporting.

Any obstacle existing to limit cooperating witnesses should be invalid. Corruption cannot be the rule and society cannot reach to the point of accepting it as something natural. For instance, there have been developed diverse international treaties related to corruption and the protection of witnesses of such crimes.[54] This seems to suggest that there is an international concern in this field.

On 2 November 2016, Argentina enacted Law No. 27.304 that replaced article 41 *ter* of the Criminal Code and broadened the spectrum of applicability of the legal figure of the cooperating witness.[55] At present, this has allowed to reduce the penalty to the level of an attempt if, during his trial, the defendant offers relevant information related to certain offences such as drug trafficking,

---

53 Resolucion 27/2018. Ver: https://www.argentina.gob.ar/sites/default/files/lineamientos_para_la_implementacion.pdf; pag 42 sobre política de no represalias a denunciantes.

54 Art. 24 of the UN Convention against Transnational Organized Crime, the Inter-American Convention against Corruption, and the United Nations Convention against Corruption in Article 33, 37(1), and Art. 37(2).

55 Files 1331-D-2016 initiated by Deputies Sergio Massa and Graciela Camaño; files 1345-D-2016 initiated by Monfort and Agostino and law projects of Deputies Garrido, Gutiérrez y Olivares, Carrizo an others – Donde Perez and others; Negri; Mestre y Petri y Cobos, Caviglia y Guistozzi – were considered as to enact this law.

customs offences, terrorism, child pornography offenses, unlawful association, and offences against public administration.

The new law regulates procedural aspects of this institute by stipulating that the agreement should be performed before the investigation phase is closed and it is sent to trial. The responsibility of negotiation belongs to the prosecutor and the judge is in charge of the approval, always safekeeping the criminal guarantees of the accused person.

Another important aspect is the content of article 15 of Law No. 27.304, which stipulates that the criminal conviction of an accused and collaborator cannot "only" be based on his own declarations. In other words, a final decision should be arrived after an adversary proceeding in conformity with the rules of constructive criticism, the necessary inculpatory evidence, the accusation and the guiltiness of the accused person.

These new incentives programs allow us to identify some particular situations. There could be accused collaborators who are finally found guilty, others who are declared innocent. Witnesses who are not accused at a particular trial are the only ones excluded from this system.

In our procedural system, accusation represents a preliminary stage of commitment with a certain criminal investigation. This program has been created with the aim of introducing an incentive with the capability to break the traditional dichotomy that an accused person faces when submitted to a trial: *the risk of a conviction versus the risk of an acquittal.*

This new option offered by article 41 *ter* implies that an individual who knows his guiltiness could be convicted with a penal range reduced to an attempt scenario. He could even be declared innocent if the judge is not able to assess his responsibility on any other basis than his declaration (article 15). This means that an accused collaborator person can cooperate with evidence which jeopardizes other accused individuals without compromising himself – except for his own declarations. – It is an accused guilty person designing his defense by involving others and avoiding his own guiltiness, with the security that he will not be convicted with a major penalty than the one stipulated for an attempt scenario.

Another possible scenario is that of an accused person that despite of considering himself as innocent, he must face a trial and decides to cooperate to exercise his material defense. In this case the cooperator (article 41 *ter*), if convicted, he will be punished with the maximum penalty range for the offense. If he is found innocent, his cooperation would have been useful for a defense strategy which involves third parties an proves his innocence.

The new system incorporates a risk cap, a maximum limit to the penalty. It constitutes an incentive to assume a commitment of cooperation with a limited risk of a penalty that in the majority of cases admits a suspended conviction or the possibility to remain in liberty during the process and even after its culmination. According to article 26 of the Argentinian Criminal Code, this type of behaviors after the commission of an offence has a positive impact on the judges.

In conclusion, this institute should be considered as part of the full exercise of the right to a legal defense and as a useful tool to effectively resist the coercion immersed in the criminal persecution. In the case of an acquittal, there will not be a full conclusion of an agreement – at the oral trial – as the cooperation would only be useful in the analyzed terms.

These options – incentives – broaden the traditional spectrum of possibilities offered to the accused – to confess or to deny his participation in the criminal conduct –, with the risk of being convicted to a maximum penalty without any risk cap. As it was explained, with these negotiations the cost of the process could significantly drop in a case of criminal conviction.

In Argentina, since its introduction into the Criminal Code, the legal figure of the cooperating witness started to be applied in cases of corruption. The case with greater impact[56] involved dozens of entrepreneurs dedicated to the construction and high rank public officers from the National Executive Power.

Both first instance judge and the appeals chamber consolidated the constitutionality of this figure and its applicability in that case.

Moreover, in a recent leading case, one of the divisions of the Federal Chamber of Criminal "Cassation" also consolidated the legal figure of the cooperating witness.[57] Other division would be questioning its validity at the request of diverse defense lawyers of accused individuals (public officers). They required the annulment of the sentence on the base of the violation of the right to legal defense and the lack of appropriate means of registration of the recordings of the confessions of the cooperating witness (article 6 of the Law No. 27.304). This grievance is still under review, but it could motivate the intervention of the Supreme Court of Argentina.

This means that our maximum courts are still determining the applicability of this tool in the fight against corruption.

56 Case CFP 9608/2018/174/CA41, named "Fernández, Cristina Elisabet y otros s/legajo de apelación", Court N° 11 – Secretaría N° 21 – See: https://www.cij.gov.ar/nota-32935-La-C-mara-Criminal-y-Correccional-Federal-confirm--procesamientos-en-una-causa-por-corrupci-n-.html.

57 See CFP 13816/2018, "Imputado: Fernandez, Cristina Elisabet y otros s/cohecho y aceptación de dádiva testigo de identidad reservada: NN y otros, delito: cohecho aceptación de dadiva, Cámara Federal de Casación Penal – Sala 3 Fiscal: Mario Albert Villar Fiscalía ante la Cámara Federal de Casación Penal n° 1".

3.7 *Conclusion*

To sum up, it is necessary to reaffirm the idea that the decision to cooperate is an essential part of the "freedom speech",[58] as also it is the autonomy of the individual to decide the final destiny of a criminal process in which he is accused. It means the full exercise of the individual will, the only limit relies in other's liberties.

Under the post-positivism theories, John Rawls affirms that it is necessary to start from a hypothetical situation of equality and set the principles under which everyone is agreed on.[59] According to him, two rights emerge from this ideal situation, freedom of expression and religious freedom.

Starting from this, everyone should progress on behalf of his own merit, while the State should only aim at reducing inequalities. The contract is based on the individual will and reciprocity.

Under these theories, the right to freedom of expression emerges as a primordial manifestation of that autonomy and paternalistic corrections of the State are only admitted in cases of alterations to the egalitarian balance.

Human beings deserve respect for its human condition, and they cannot be used as mere instruments to a further end.[60] When a person decides, the decision is conditioned by external determinations. Acting with liberty means an autonomous manner of doing it, in conformity with a given right and not as mere instruments. Kant respects the dignity of the human only because its human condition and by doing so he combines moral, liberty and reason.

Finally, from a theory of punishment's perspective, we agree with Jackobs when he points that these forms of solving conflicts – specially in a guiltiness assumption and a contribution of evidence to the *ius puniendi* – implies a clear sign of reaffirmation of the validity of the norm, the crucial aim of punishment.

It is an undeniable argument that brings legitimacy to the institute of cooperation. The contribution starts from a premise of recognition. This is the condition of an accused person of a certain offence and his will to end this conflict in a diverse manner, different from criminal punishment. Unequivocally, this implies the reaffirmation of the validity of a legal system that sustains social harmony.

---

58 The European Court of Human Rights in the case "Guja vs. Maldova" (Application No. 14 277 /04, February 12, 2008).

59 Rawls, J., op. cit.

60 Kant, Immanuel, *Fundamentación de la Metafísica de las Costumbres*, Ed. Barbosa, Puerto Rico, 2007, pp. 41/42.

With or without regret, the individual tries to rectify his deviated action to another channel in conformity with the social contract.[61]

It is necessary to avoid falling into those dialectical traps that lead us to believe that composition systems can be illegals for attempting against the constitutional pillars of the criminal process.

On the contrary, cooperation is an institute already used in ancient criminal regimes and represents a direct externalization of the autonomy of the will principle of the human being.

Its appropriate regulation does not constitute *per se* any attempt to the constitutional structure of criminal and procedural law. It does not violate the right to a fair trial, not even the due process or the equality of arms. Obviously, there should be certain counterweights in its application in order to guarantee the relative autonomy of others.

Finally, the system of cooperation is a possible and necessary consequence of an accusatory system, with full validity of the principle of opportunity. As the prosecutor is in charge of evaluating the contribution of evidence and decides the level of forgiveness to the accused, we enter into a particular area of selection of cases which deserve a treatment which is different from the mere imposition of a penalty.

With regard to the factors that could affect the willingness of the act (benefits stipulated by the State), we believe the solution must be made on the basis of the autonomy principle. Paternalistic positions, which are highly used to justify state intervention, should be left aside.

An individual submitted to trial, with previous fulfillment of all the required formalities, should be able to decide to cooperate with the prosecutor thesis. It is an essential part of his condition of an autonomous human being who exercise his right to defense according to his best convenience and counselling. He performs his right to freedom of expression and opinion, and he is not responsible for explaining internal valuable judgments – even speculative – that lead to act in that sense.

As it was explained, the only unbridgeable limit is the relative autonomy of others.

At this point, it is essential to notice that an accused person who adopts this role does not turn into a "undercover prosecutor". It means he is still an accused person who has chosen a certain procedural strategy of cooperation with the judicial authorities; he remains being an accused person and his performance is limited to incorporate evidence to the proceeding.

61 Rousseau, Jean Jacques, *The Social Contrat, or principles of political right* (1762). *Translated by G.D.H. Cole, public domain Foederis æquas Dicamus leges. Virgil, Æneid x.*

Any subjective consideration issued by the cooperation about the criminal responsibility of others lacks relevancy if it is not based on other evidence. The completion of the truth is an exclusive responsibility of the owner of the public accusation.[62]

The cooperator only provides with new evidence that should be substantiated by the prosecutor. If this evidence is not verified, the cooperation would not be useful and consequently, there will not benefits from that cooperation.

This manner of exercising the right to legal defense does not suppose the violation of the principle of equality of arms in the process. Each part continues to perform their role and the only newness is that of the strategy of defense from one of the accused individuals, which generates a new source of evidence.

The rest of the accused persons who decide not to support this strategy can continue to resist the content and veracity of the new incorporated evidence. They are able to interrogate witnesses, to participate in irreproducible proceedings, to propose their own witnesses, they also have the possibility to contest those witnesses who are biased under their criteria, etc.

The rights of others are not violated due to the intervention of a cooperator. As it was previously developed here, only the amount and quality of evidence is altered and it is still subject to the same general rules of scrutiny.

In conclusion, our responsibility is to stimulate people to abide by the law and to enforce the law. We therefore need to:

- give incentives to potential whistleblowers, victims and cooperating witnesses.
- create a new legislation to protect their rights.
- create a reliable system to receive their testimonies.
- create a rewards system to ensure their cooperation.
- control the interrelations between all actors (this should be the main responsibility of the Justice System) and monitor the networking (this should be the main responsibility of the civil society).
- train all the actors of the judicial system in order to put an end to the stigmatization of whistleblowers, victims, and cooperating witnesses.

In our American countries, these people have negative incentives to collaborate with justice. In fact, these people are encouraged to work for mafias that ensure them protection and money.

Therefore, it is essential to modify the incentive system in favor of people that have substantial information to contribute with justice. In Argentina, these people are only encouraged to remain in silence.

62 Maier, op. cit., pp. 581/2.

The most modern tool to fight against corruption includes a cooperation system between citizens and governments.

We must encourage countries to introduce a comprehensive legislation on whistleblowers and cooperating witnesses to protect those that speak out and to ensure that their claims are properly investigated. Companies, public agencies and non-profit organizations should introduce mechanisms for internal reporting. In addition, workplace reprisals against these people should be seen as another form of corruption.

After all, when witnesses of corruption offences feel confident to report these scenarios, corrupt individuals cannot hide behind the walls of silence.

www.ingramcontent.com/pod-product-compliance
Lightning Source LLC
Chambersburg PA
CBHW031329230926
51848CB00001B/160
9789004459809